ChristWise

Discipleship Guide for Youth

Troy Fitzgerald

REVIEW AND HERALD® PUBLISHING ASSOCIATION
HAGERSTOWN, MD 21740

The author assumes full responsibility for the accuracy of all facts and quotations as cited in this book.

Unless otherwise noted, Bible texts credited to NIV are from the *Holy Bible, New International Version.* Copyright ©
1973, 1978, 1984, International Bible Society. Used by permission of Zondervan Bible Publishers.

This book was
Edited by Gerald Wheeler
Copyedited by Delma Miller and James Cavil
Designed by Tina M. Ivany
Electronic makeup by Shirley M. Bolivar
Cover photo by PhotoDisc
Typeset: Veljovic 12/16

PRINTED IN U.S.A.

06 05 04 03 02   5 4 3 2 1

R&H Cataloging Service
Fitzgerald, Troy, 1968-
    ChristWise

    1. Seventh-day Adventist—Doctrines   I. Title.

            268.433

ISBN 0-8280-1712-3

Other books by Troy Fitzgerald:

ChristWise: Discipleship Guide for Juniors
ChristWise: Discipleship Guide for Teens
ChristWise: Leader's Guide for Juniors, Teens, and Youth

To order, call 1-800-765-6955.
Visit us at www.reviewandherald.com for information on other Review and Herald® products.

If this book belongs to you, then it may be because you have made the decision to be baptized or are seriously thinking about it. Congratulations! There are several truths about baptism and preparing for baptism that are important to understand. Know first and foremost that while many people may be proud of you for taking this step, no one is more excited about your decision to follow Christ in baptism than the Father in heaven. Baptism represents the following wonderful things.

1. It signifies a desire to be born again (John 3:1-6; John 1:10-12).

2. It is a confession and asking for forgiveness of sins (Acts 2:38; Mark 1:5-9).

3. Through it the Father announces that we rightfully belong to Him (Mark 1:10-12).

4. It indicates death to the old self and the embrace of a new life (Romans 6:1-6).

5. We become part of a church family (1 Corinthians 12:13).

6. All heaven rejoices (Luke 15:7).

Repentance and baptism. Repentance simply means to "change your mind and turn your steps the other direction." People who want to be baptized usually have experienced a heartfelt desire to surrender their life to Christ and live fully for Him. As you continue to grow in God's grace it is my sincere hope that you will learn the great truths of Scripture and live in the certainty and joy of a relationship with the Savior.

ChristWise **is** a journey through the teachings of the Seventh-day Adventist Church as portrayed in the life of Christ. It is our belief that Christ is the source and center of all of Scripture and that the doctrines describe the many ways

God's character and His love permeate this world of sin. The lessons rest on several building blocks.

1. Christ wants us to know Him personally, not just facts about the Bible. To know what day the Sabbath is or what happens to a person's body at death is important only as it emerges from the person of Jesus. Adventist faith involves a deep abiding knowledge and walk with Jesus.

2. Young people can actively study, experience, and live in ways that serve as examples to other believers. Since we learn best by doing, we have designed the lessons so that you can learn together with a partner as well as experience the Christian life individually.

3. Other people are important in the learning process. The *ChristWise* approach seeks to integrate young people with those who can serve not just as teachers, but as mentors—friends who join the journey of discipleship with you. The experiences and ideas of others in your congregation are significant tools for learning as well.

ChristWise **will** engage your heart and mind in a variety of ways:

Open Questions: It includes questions that seek to get us thinking. Questions that prompt more than a yes or no from us. They encourage us to take a stand, to tell a story, and to make a choice. An open question fosters good thinking.

Opening Story: The lessons contain a short story or illustration that opens up the topic by getting to the heart of the issue. Such stories can make us laugh, cry, or even get mad. The opening story launches you into the study in which you can then approach the Word with a thoughtful mind.

Life of Christ: A section from Christ's teachings or a story from His life creates the perfect backdrop for the teachings of the Adventist faith. The lessons have as their goal discovering the many ways in which He tried to portray God's great plan for humanity.

We Believe: A statement of faith rooted in Scripture, it seeks to deepen your understanding and your knowledge of the Bible by encouraging you to mark up your Bible in a way that will help you to witness to someone else.

Way to Pray: Praying to God is like breathing. The lessons will prepare you to move beyond clichés to enable you to pray to God with power and sincerity. You will learn to pray about things that you never talked to God about before.

More Than Words: Take time to listen to people tell their stories. They will share their insights and ideas as you interview them with questions that will probe to the heart of the matter.

In the Mirror: Honestly looking inside our hearts and minds is a good way to grow up in Christ. Reflecting on how you have learned and what you think makes you morally and spiritually strong.

A few final tips before you start the journey:

Communicate clearly with your partner about the meeting time, expectations, and the things each of you need to bring.

Make this study a priority for you. Sometimes you may be tempted to sleep or watch TV instead of doing the work in this book. Commit yourself and your partner to remain faithful.

Don't breeze over any of the parts of this study. If you fall behind, save it for later. It is better to do just a little and do it thoughtfully than to rush through the whole study without letting it get into your heart and mind.

Be thinking about how you might become someone who is a leader/teacher or a mentor for someone else in the future.

The Scriptures

Open Questions

Have you ever had to send a message to another person but been unable to do so because of a communication mess-up? How did you feel? Share the story.

Suppose you have a 12-year-old child. You have two minutes to pass on to him or her information that will be most helpful for their future survival and happiness. What will you say? (Write out your advice.)

Opening Story

I'm not a sensational guy when I speak to young people. One time, though, I couldn't resist the urge to be edgy. As I began the sermon I announced, "Enough of this—this is so ridiculous! What are we all doing here, anyway? What does this book have to say that's relevant to us?" I began ripping random pages out of my Bible, crumpling them roughly and throwing them to the ground. I even had the guts to stomp irreverently on a few crumpled pages beneath my feet.

Talk about getting their attention! Gasps exploded through the chapel like gunshots on a battlefield. Students gazed at me in horror, amazed by my blasphemous treatment of the Sacred Scriptures. Older adults in the back of the room began murmuring about how to get rid of me before I inflicted any further damage on innocent young minds.

"Relax," I said finally. "Anyone who knows me knows I would never tear up a Bible. I simply took a cheap Harlequin romance novel and put an old Bible cover on it." (I have no problem defacing romance novels.) The tension eased a little, but before I lost the crowd's attention, I posed a question to the squirming group: "Which is worse—openly defacing God's Word or quietly ignoring it day by day?"

It is a shocking way to approach the Scriptures, but think about the words John penned years ago. The Bible writers chose the sayings and stories of the Bible because they communicate what is vital to know about God.

Life of Christ

John 20:24-31

"Now Thomas (called Didymus), one of the Twelve, was not with the disciples when Jesus came. So the other disciples told him, 'We have seen the Lord!' But he said to them, 'Unless I see the nail marks in his hands and put my finger where the nails were, and put my hand into his side, I will not believe it.' A week later his disciples were in the house again, and Thomas was with them. Though the doors were locked, Jesus came and stood among them and said, 'Peace be with you!' Then he said to Thomas, 'Put your finger here; see my hands. Reach out your hand and put it into my side. Stop doubting and believe.' Thomas said to him, 'My Lord and my God!' Then Jesus told him, 'Because you have seen me, you have believed; blessed are those who have not seen and yet have believed.' Jesus did many other miraculous signs in the presence of his disciples, which are not recorded in this book. But these are written that you may believe that Jesus is the Christ, the Son of God, and that by believing you may have life in his name."

We Believe

The Scriptures

"The Holy Scriptures . . . are the written Word of God, given by divine inspiration through holy men of God who spoke and wrote as they were moved by the Holy Spirit."* Everything we need for salvation is available in the Bible. The Bible is really about God revealing to us who He is and who we are in relation to Him. It reveals a trustworthy picture of God and becomes the authoritative guide for people as they follow Him.

Read the following verses and briefly paraphrase them in your own words. Don't use the same words or phrases as the text—be creative!

a. 2 Peter 1:20, 21

b. 2 Timothy 3:16

c. Hebrews 1:1, 2

d. Hebrews 4:12

e. John 5:39

f. Psalm 119:105

g. Proverbs 30:5

h. 1 Thessalonians 2:13

i. James 1:22-25

Which verses above especially speak to you about God's Word in your life? Why?

I Believe

(Write what you believe about the Bible based on your study so far.)

Way to Pray

"Your word is a lamp to my feet and a light for my path" (Psalm 119:105).
Write a prayer to God about a part of your life that really needs insight and guidance from His Word.

More Than Words

Interview someone you know about his or her experience in trusting God's Word. Here are a few questions to ask them:

1. When in your life did you come to trust the Bible as God's Word for you?
2. When has the Bible been a real source of strength to you? Have you had times when you had doubts about God's Word?
3. If you could tell only one story from Scripture, which one would you choose to help a friend know God? Why?

Soil Check

What soil represents your life the most (Matthew 13:3-8; 18-23)? How can you make the soil of your heart more receptive to God's Word in your life?

In the Mirror

If God has only two minutes to get a message through to you on paper, write what you think He might say to you—keeping in mind what you know about the purpose, person, and power of His Word.

---

* *Seventh-day Adventists Believe*, p. 4.

The Trinity

Open Questions

Which member of the Trinity (Father, Son, Holy Spirit) do you relate to the most? Why?

How do you think your best friend would describe you? How well do you think they know you? On the continuum below, indicate the degree at which the person who knows you the best really understands you.

1—Knows very little of the real you
5—Knows you completely

1	2	3	4	5

Knows very little   **Knows you completely**

How would you like to be Moses and get this response from God?

"Moses said to God, 'Suppose I go to the Israelites and say to them,

"The God of your fathers has sent me to you," and they ask me, "What is his name?" Then what shall I tell them?' God said to Moses, 'I AM WHO I AM. This is what you are to say to the Israelites: "I AM has sent me to you"'" (Exodus 3:13, 14).

"I AM." What kind of answer is that? Why does this have to be such a mystery?

Just give me a nice, neat definition of who You are and what I should call You and we'll be OK, you may be thinking to yourself. But God reveals not only what we *need* to know but what we *can* know. Why the mystery? It is not because God is hiding. He is using every way possible to make His character clear to us. In looking at who God is, it is important to note two facts: 1. God has revealed Himself plainly enough that we can love and serve Him. 2. God's desire is to reveal more of Him to us personally each day.

Opening Story

When a group of us were in Africa holding meetings and conducting a free medical clinic, Jaci prayed a remarkable prayer. Exhausted from the constant drain on her strength and her spirit, she begged, "God, I don't feel like I have anything to give today. Father, lend me Your heart today, and I will give that away."

While Jaci doesn't claim to know all about God, she knew enough about Him to recognize that she needed Him at that moment. Maybe all she knew was that God was the great "I AM"—and that would be enough. For the rest of the day her service to others mattered more than her own comfort, more than her inner cares and conflicting emotions. If you had asked her, she would not have claimed to know everything about God, nor would she have said she was always close to Him. But she knew enough about God to know what He is like: selfless, compassionate, and heartbroken at the sight of suffering people. The list of His traits could go on and on. Why? Because God is still revealing who He is to us. But for the moment, compassion and selfless service can become the way to live. Jaci has never been the same since that experience.

The Trinity is a word to describe God—the Father, Son, and Holy Spirit. Like us, God has personality. He has a character. But all we can know about Him is what He reveals to us. The problem with understanding the Trinity comes when we try to define or completely explain or describe the nature, personality, and person of God. Instead of "figuring it out," try letting God reveal Himself to you through His Word. Let Him show His heart to you. You will be confused if you focus on the "what" of the Trinity, but you will find yourself changed when you see the who of the Trinity.

Life of Christ

Matthew 28:18-20

"Then Jesus came to them and said, 'All authority in heaven and on earth has been given to me. Therefore go and make disciples of all nations, baptizing them in the name of the Father and of the Son and of the Holy Spirit, and teaching them to obey everything I have commanded you. And surely I am with you always, to the very end of the age.'"

We Believe

The Trinity

"There is one God: Father, Son, and Holy Spirit, a unity of co-eternal Persons. God is immortal, all-powerful, all-knowing, above all, and ever present. He is infinite and beyond human comprehension, yet known through His self-revelation. He is forever worthy of worship, adoration, and service by the whole creation."[1]

Read the following verses and briefly paraphrase them in your own words. Think about what they say about who God is and what we can know about Him.

    a. Deuteronomy 6:4

    b. Matthew 28:19, 20

    c. 2 Corinthians 13:14

The Father

"God the Eternal Father is the Creator, Source, Sustainer, and Sovereign of all creation. He is just and holy, merciful and gracious, slow to anger, and abounding in steadfast love and faithfulness. The qualities and powers exhibited in the Son and the Holy Spirit are also revelations of the Father." [2]

Read the following verses and briefly paraphrase their meaning in your own words. How does God's Word describe the Father?

    a. Genesis 1:1

    b. John 3:16

    c. John 14:8-11

As you have read and marked the verses in your Bible, what three characteristics of God the Father are most meaningful to you right now? Which passages describe those qualities?

The Son

"God the Eternal Son became incarnate in Jesus Christ. Through Him all things were created, the character of God is revealed, the salvation of humanity is accomplished, and the world is judged. Forever truly God, He became also truly man, Jesus the Christ. He was conceived of the Holy Spirit and born of the virgin Mary. He lived and experienced temptation as a human being, but perfectly exemplified the righteousness and love of God. By His miracles He manifested God's power and was attested as God's promised Messiah. He suffered and died voluntarily on the cross for our sins and in our place, was raised from the dead, and ascended to minister in the heavenly sanctuary in our behalf. He will come again in glory for the final deliverance of His people and the restoration of all things." [3]

    a. John 1:1-3, 14

    b. Luke 1:35

    c. Colossians 1:13-20

    d. John 10:30

As you have read and marked the verses in your Bible, which three characteristics of God the Son are most meaningful to you right now? Which passages best describe those qualities?

The Holy Spirit

"God the eternal Spirit was active with the Father and the Son in Creation, incarnation, and redemption. He inspired the writers of Scripture. He filled Christ's life with power. He draws and convicts human beings; and those who respond He renews and transforms into the image of God. Sent by the Father and the Son to be always with His children, He extends spiritual gifts to the church, empowers it to bear witness to Christ, and in harmony with the Scriptures leads it into all truth."[4]

a. Genesis 1:1, 2

b. John 14:16-18, 26

c. Acts 1:8

d. Ephesians 4:11, 12

As you have read and marked the verses in your Bible, which three characteristics of God the Holy Spirit are most meaningful to you? Now note which passages describe those qualities.

Think about how you would describe the person and the work of the Holy Spirit to a child. What illustrations or analogies would you use?

Way to Pray

Write a prayer to each person of the Trinity based upon what you know about Them. Ask God to reveal Himself more fully to you this week.

More Than Words

Interview: Invite someone you know who has thought and studied about the Trinity to share with you in a short interview. Ask them:

How do you describe the different members of the Trinity? What other ways might you explain Their relationship? Why do you think the Bible describes God in these three ways/personalities?

In the Mirror

Take a few moments to reflect on what you discovered this week about the Trinity that you had not understood before. What do you want to say to God today about who you think He is?

---

[1] *Seventh-day Adventists Believe,* p. 16.
[2] *Ibid.,* p. 28.
[3] *Ibid.,* p. 36.
[4] *Ibid.,* p. 58.

The Great Controversy

Open Questions

Would people characterize you as a strong-willed person, or are you more laid-back and easygoing? What do you think are some strengths and weaknesses of both personality types?

1—I live each day aware of the war between good and evil.
5—I rarely consider the reality of supernatural warfare taking place.

1	2	3	4	5
Aware				**Rarely think about it**

Opening Story

My son looked back over his shoulder to the kids screaming and chasing each other on the playground. He came to report the current status of the battle that raged between two groups on the playground. "The girls are trying to get us," my son proudly sputtered, "and I'm a bad guy!" Then he watched to see my reaction to his self-proclaimed status as a bad boy.

I smiled. "Go get 'em, bad guy!" He was already off to the war. Immediately three girls captured and placed him in "jail." But he didn't seem to mind, and I didn't blame him. It was a game. Being the "bad guy" was part of the game. After all, it is only a game, right? Good girls and bad guys?

My son always wants to be the bad guy. I'll be honest with you—that worries me a bit. Why? Bad guys are, well, bad. Real life isn't a playground. As we go through our daily routine, there is an all-out war raging all around us, with real people and real casualties. At the end of the day it is not as easy as shaking off the dust of the playground and going home to have a sandwich and a "tubby." Probably the most dangerous attitude to have in a time of war is the misguided notion that there is no war, no danger, and no side on which to take a stand.

Jesus entered the war zone when He was born. But His visit to the wilderness to prepare for His ministry is a special point at which the battle between Christ and Satan intensified. Look at the great controversy between Christ and Satan in the desert wilderness, and consider what this war is about as you watch the two armies clash.

Life of Christ

Luke 4:1-13

"Jesus, full of the Holy Spirit, returned from the Jordan and was led by the Spirit in the desert, where for forty days he was tempted by the devil. He ate nothing during those days, and at the end of them he was hungry. The devil said to him, 'If you are the Son of God, tell this stone to become bread.' Jesus answered, 'It is written: "Man does not live on bread alone."' The devil led him up to a high place and showed him in an instant all the kingdoms of the world. And he said to him, 'I will give you all their authority and splendor, for it has been given to me, and I can give it to anyone I want to. So if you worship me, it will all be yours.' Jesus answered, 'It is written: "Worship the Lord your God and serve him only."' The devil led him to Jerusalem and had him stand on the highest point of the temple. 'If you are the Son of God,' he said, 'throw yourself down from here. For it is written: "He will command his angels concerning you to guard you carefully; they will lift you up in their hands, so that you will not strike your foot against a stone."' Jesus answered, 'It says: "Do not put the Lord your God to the test."' When the devil had finished all this tempting, he left him until an opportune time."

Mark 8:27-33

"Jesus and his disciples went on to the villages around Caesarea Philippi. On the way he asked them, 'Who do people say I am?' They replied, 'Some say John the Baptist; others say Elijah; and still others, one of the prophets.' 'But what about you?' he asked. 'Who do you say I am?' Peter answered, 'You are the Christ.' Jesus warned them not to tell anyone about him. He then began to teach them that the Son of Man must suffer many things and be rejected by the elders, chief priests and teachers of the law, and that he must be killed and after three days rise again. He spoke plainly about this, and Peter took him aside and began to rebuke him. But when Jesus turned and looked at his disciples, he rebuked Peter. 'Get behind me, Satan!' he said. 'You do not have in mind the things of God, but the things of men.'"

Mark 14:32-38

"They went to a place called Gethsemane, and Jesus said to his disciples, 'Sit here while I pray.' He took Peter, James and John along with him, and he began to be deeply distressed and troubled. 'My soul is overwhelmed with sorrow to the point of death,' he said to them. 'Stay here and keep watch.' Going a little farther, he fell to the ground and prayed that if possible the hour might pass from him. 'Abba, Father,' he said, 'everything is possible for you. Take this cup from me. Yet not what I will, but what you will.' Then he returned to his disciples and found them sleeping. 'Simon,' he said to Peter, 'are you asleep? Could you not keep watch for one hour? Watch and pray so that you will not fall into temptation. The spirit is willing, but the body is weak.'"

Matthew 27:39-43

"Those who passed by hurled insults at him, shaking their heads and saying, 'You who are going to destroy the temple and build it in three days, save yourself! Come down from the cross, if you are the Son of God!' In the same way the chief priests, the teachers of the law and the elders mocked him. 'He saved others,' they said, 'but he can't save himself! He's the King of Israel! Let him come down now from the cross, and we will believe in him. He trusts in God. Let God rescue him now if he wants him, for he said, "I am the Son of God."' "

Divide this study between you and your partner. Each of you should take a story and ask the following questions:

1. Underline or circle the verse you think is key to understanding this story.
2. Describe the struggle taking place in this story.
3. How is the adversary at war with Jesus? What is Satan seeking to accomplish?
4. How does Jesus respond, and why do you think He responds this way?
5. How do these stories depict the great controversy? According to these stories, what is the great controversy really about? (Restrict your answer to a sentence.)

Share responses to the questions, then work on the following questions together:

1. What temptation does Satan constantly throw at Jesus?
2. How would you describe Jesus' response to these dilemmas? What is His attitude?
3. In a sentence or two, tell what God's will was in the garden when Jesus said, "Not My will, but Yours . . ."
4. What do you think it will take for us (you) to be able to offer that prayer in any situation? Under what circumstance is it most difficult for you to surrender your will to God's?

We Believe

The Great Controversy

The great controversy juts out of the landscape of the life of Christ like giant rocks thrusting from the ground. The war between Christ and Satan is and always will be about self versus selflessness.

It's a war of the wills—your will versus the will of God.

"All humanity is now involved in a great controversy between Christ and Satan regarding the character of God, His law, and His sovereignty over the universe. This conflict originated in heaven when a created being, endowed with freedom of choice, in self-exaltation became Satan, God's adversary, and led into rebellion a portion of the angels. He introduced the spirit of rebellion into this world when he led Adam and Eve into sin. This human sin resulted in the distortion of the image of God in humanity, the disordering of the created world, and its eventual devastation at the time of the worldwide flood. Observed by the whole creation, this world became the arena of the universal conflict, out of which the God of love will ultimately be vindicated. To assist His people in this controversy, Christ sends the Holy Spirit and the loyal angels to guide, protect, and sustain them in the way of salvation."*

a. Revelation 12:4-9
b. Isaiah 14:12-14
c. Ezekiel 28:12-18
d. Genesis 3
e. Genesis 6–8
f. 2 Peter 3:6
g. 1 Corinthians 4:9

Which verse spoke to you most profoundly about the conflict between Christ and Satan? Why?

As you mark (chain-reference) your Bible with these passages, what one word do you find that best describes the problem of the great controversy?

I Believe

How would you answer someone who asks, "How can I believe or serve a God who allows the innocent to suffer and the guilty to go unpunished?"

As you look at what Scripture says about how sin began and how God chooses to deal with it, how would you explain what you find to someone who doesn't know much about the Bible?

Way to Pray

When you pray "Father, Your will be done, not mine," be specific with God about the things that seem to be His will and the things that you want.

More Than Words

Jesus chose to do His Father's will and His Father's way—alone in the desert, in conflict with a close friend, in the heat of a big decision, in front of the world at Calvary. Alone. Among friends.

Facing big decisions. As you consider the decisions and struggles you will have to face in your life, think of tangible ways to remind yourself that you are caught in a spiritual war. Keep them visible and practical. I'm putting bright-blue tape on the tips of my running shoes so when I jog (alone) I'll be reminded of My Father's will for my life. By my phone (where I make decisions) I have taped to the desk: "Not my will, but Yours." You can create your own reminders. The Old Testament is filled with symbols that stayed in the memories of believers so they would not forget.

Interview: Ask someone how they would deal with this dilemma:

Many people have a difficult time relating to a God who seems either unwilling or unable to respond to the bad things that happen to innocent people in the world. How do you explain a loving God to people when so many innocent people suffer? How do I relate to a God who seems far away or distant?

In the Mirror

In what ways do you see the great controversy at work in your life? in those around you? Reflect on either how oblivious or aware you are of this struggle between good and evil, of the war between human will and God's will.

---

* *Seventh-day Adventists Believe,* p. 98.

The Experience of Salvation

Open Questions

When in your life have you felt as if you were the furthest away from God? What helped you draw close to Him in those moments?

Opening Story

"That's life." It was one of her favorite sayings, a common phrase when things turned out less desirable than she wanted or expected. I knew her only from the little statements she made in front of her friends in the ice-cream shop I worked in while I was in high school. Sabrina was a few years younger than I was, but she still scared me. Always dressed in black, her dyed black hair hung like a greasy curtain covering her eyes. Although she rarely spoke, when she did, her words displayed what her hair tried to hide—her life was empty, even hopeless.

I would try to avoid being the one to say to Sabrina, "May I help you?" Although I managed to dodge that experience several times during the summer, on one occasion I did get stuck with her. She ordered her ice cream—two scoops of Black Forest chocolate. When I handed the ice-cream cone to her I stared at her wrists as she reached for the ice cream. Her long sleeves slid back to reveal a tattoo on the inside of each forearm—a razor blade. Who would tattoo a razor blade on their wrists? Sabrina would and did. Instinctively I jumped, the ice-cream cone tipped, and the awkward, terrible moment continued as I had to remake her ice cream.

Later in the year I was able to actually have a conversation with her. As the store was closing one night, I asked her about her tattoos. "I don't know," she said. "I think about killing myself a lot, but I don't have the guts—so I got a tattoo instead. My life hasn't been so great. That's life, I guess."

I wish I could say that I prayed for her, or with her. But I didn't. I was just as lost as she was—I just didn't know it. I returned to the ice-cream shop two years later while visiting in my hometown. As I studied the familiar tubs of ice cream in the window I heard that familiar phrase: "May I help you?" I looked up—it was Sabrina. But not the one I used to know. For the first time ever I think I saw her eyes. I almost didn't believe it was she. We talked as she prepared my ice-cream sundae. "Sabrina, what happened?" I had to ask. She described how she met Christ through a friend, and now she was trying to put her life back together. When I glanced at her arms I saw that they bore the evidence of the painful surgery to remove the tattoos. She smiled. "Did it hurt?"

"Yeah, but that's life." She said it with a sense of peace this time, making me believe that the phrase meant something different. As I left the store with a new confidence in God's power to completely restore someone's life, I began thinking about having Him transform mine.

Many times Jesus describes the gift of salvation as "life." Scripture describes the experience of conversion as a birth:

"Yet to all who received him, to those who believed in his name, he gave the right to become children of God—children born not of natural descent, nor of human decision or a husband's will, but born of God" (John 1:12, 13).

Such a birth is usually the result of the power of God's message of salvation through His Word:

"For you have been born again, not of perishable seed, but of imperishable, through the living and enduring word of God" (1 Peter 1:23).

"He chose to give us birth through the word of truth, that we might be a kind of firstfruits of all he created" (James 1:18).

"That's life." Or "Now, that's *the* life." Apply these two expressions about life to this story from the life of Christ in which Jesus demonstrates in a marvelous way the experience of salvation in the restoration of a man dying with leprosy.

Life of Christ

Mark 1:40-45

"A man with leprosy came to him and begged him on his knees, 'If you are willing, you can make me clean.' Filled with compassion, Jesus reached out his hand and touched the man. 'I am willing,' he said. 'Be clean!' Immediately the leprosy left him and he was cured. Jesus sent him away at once with a strong warning: 'See that you don't tell this to anyone. But go, show yourself to the priest and offer the sacrifices that Moses commanded for your cleansing, as a testimony to them.' Instead he went out and began to talk freely, spreading the news. As a result, Jesus could no longer enter a town openly but stayed outside in lonely places. Yet the people still came to him from everywhere."

How is the leper's experience with leprosy and healing like our experience with sin and salvation?

We Believe

The Experience of Salvation

"In infinite love and mercy God made Christ, who knew no sin, to be sin for us, so that in Him we might be made the righteousness of God. Led by the Holy Spirit we sense our need, acknowledge our sinfulness, repent of our transgressions, and exercise faith in Jesus as Lord and Christ, as Substitute and Example. This faith, which receives salvation, comes through the divine power of the Word and is the gift of God's grace. Through Christ we are justified, adopted as God's sons and daughters, and delivered from the lordship of sin. Through the Spirit we are born again and sanctified; the Spirit renews our minds, writes God's law of love in our hearts, and we are given the power to live a holy life. Abiding in Him we become partakers of the divine nature and have the assurance of salvation now and in the judgment."*

What do these passages say about the experience of salvation?

a. John 3:16
b. Romans 3:21
c. 2 Corinthians 5:17-21
d. Galatians 4:4-7
e. Titus 3:3-7
f. Romans 8:14-17
g. Romans 10:17
h. Galatians 3:2
i. Romans 8:1-4
j. Romans 12:2

Which passages above spoke to you the most about God's saving power? How would you describe the experience of salvation to another person? What is it, and how do you get it?

Way to Pray

Read 1 John 5:13, 14. As you pray, focus on thanking God with confidence for giving you the gift of salvation. You can write out your prayer if you want.

More Than Words

Interview: Invite someone to share their story of conversion with you. Ask them:

How did you come to give your life to Christ? What were the circumstances of your salvation experience? How do you live in a world of sin with the confidence that you are saved? How do you remind yourself of this experience?

Read Mark 5:18-20.

Tell another person this week about the certainty and the joy you have as someone who is "saved."

In the Mirror

Take a few moments to reflect. Why do you think it is difficult to experience the gift of salvation in our world today? What are the obstacles? What can we do to enable people to receive the free gift of God's grace in our busy world?

* *Seventh-day Adventists Believe,* p. 118.

Baptism

Open Questions

Agree or Disagree:

Baptism is required for those who want to be saved.

Opening Story

Birth (the experience of salvation), adoption (baptism), and marriage (the law of God) help us to understand what it means to live in a relationship with God. When we are born, we receive life. God's Word, His message of salvation, comes to us and we believe and receive it. When we are born, it is usually into a family. Since we are born sinners, we call our spiritual rebirth experience "being born again." The Bible uses the idea of adoption to describe our newfound life in God's family. (In the next lesson we will discuss marriage. Through it we begin a new family—and, I might add, become part of another.)

The Bible uses these three experiences to describe how believers relate to God and His family. This lesson is about the life-changing experience of baptism.

"After his grandmother's funeral, Gary was leafing through his grandma's well-worn Bible, and he found his name on the family register page. He expected to see his name there, but what he didn't expect to see was the word written next to his name—ADOPTED. Gary was bewildered, hurt, and not a little angry that nobody had ever told him. It wasn't the best way for him to find out how he got into the family." [1]

Adoption. I used the analogy in a sermon I gave to some young people at a retreat. A young man came to me after the closing song and said, "Thanks for the talk. But when you spoke about being God's children through adoption you never really mentioned much about what it feels like to be chosen." He was right. I missed it entirely. "I'm adopted," he continued, "and for me the best thing about being adopted is that, although my biological parents wouldn't keep me, someone did choose me. Do you understand how important it is to really experience what it is like to be chosen?" I didn't, but that night Neal helped me.

I went to the Scriptures and found this:

"For he chose us in him before the creation of the world to be holy and blameless in his sight. In love he predestined us to be adopted as his sons through Jesus Christ, in accordance with his pleasure and will—to the praise of his glorious grace, which he has freely given us in the One he loves" (Ephesians 1:4-6).

Chosen. In our sinful, fallen world, Christ uses adoption to describe our entrance into a new life in His family. He chose you. Christ declared:

"You did not choose me, but I chose you and appointed you to go and bear fruit—fruit that will last. Then the Father will give you whatever you ask in my name" (John 15:16).

Christ "chose us" before we even dreamed of choosing Him. But notice that we show our acceptance of this grace by "receiving" and "believing." John describes this experience in the context of John the Baptist inviting people to respond to the Savior by being born into the family of God. Talk with your partner about the significance of "believing and receiving" and also the "right to be called children of God."

Life of Christ

John 1:10-13

"He was in the world, and though the world was made through him, the world did not recognize him. He came to that which was his own, but his own did not receive him. Yet to all who received him, to those who believed in his name, he gave the right to become children of God—children born not of natural descent, nor of human decision or a husband's will, but born of God."

As you consider your own baptism, how does the idea of adoption and entering into a new family shape the way you think of baptism?

We Believe

Baptism

"By baptism we confess our faith in the death and resurrection of Jesus Christ, and testify of our death to sin and of our purpose to walk in newness of life. Thus we acknowledge Christ as Lord and Saviour, and become His people, and are received as members by His church. Baptism is a symbol of our union with Christ, the forgiveness of our sins, and our reception of the Holy Spirit. It is by immersion in water and is contingent on an affirmation of faith in Jesus and evidence of repentance of sin. It follows instruction in the Holy Scriptures and acceptance of their teachings." [2]

    a. Romans 6:1-6
    b. Acts 2:38

c. Acts 16:30-33

d. Acts 22:16

e. Colossians 2:12, 13

f. Matthew 28:19, 20

g. 1 Corinthians 12:13

What is your own statement of belief about baptism?

Way to Pray

Read the prayer that Jesus offers to His Father in John 17. Think about what Christ asked for as He prayed for Himself, His disciples, and for everyone who would become His disciples over time. You are one of those He prayed for 2,000 years ago. Talk to Christ in prayer about His prayer for you and consider asking for some of the same things He prayed for you as you pray this week.

More Than Words

Decide how you want your baptism to be memorable. Plan the event in such a way that it will be a meaningful statement to God and other believers about your decision: What are some things you want to happen, to be said, and to be experienced during this time?

Interview: Invite someone to share with you the significance of their baptism.

What motivated them to make the decision to be baptized?

What happened at their baptism that they will never forget?

How do they remind themselves of the meaning of their baptism?

In the Mirror

Part of baptism is entry into a church family. How do you see yourself becoming a part of the family? What do you want to do to serve as a member of God's family in your church? What will you bring to the church family that you think might be helpful to its mission?

[1] Warren Wiersbe, *Being a Child of God*, p. 21.
[2] *Seventh-day Adventists Believe,* p. 180.

Creation

Opening Story

Lost in the preschool's maze of proudly displayed construction paper portraits, I scanned the room for my son's creative handiwork. The pictures lining the walls were great. Their jagged lines and shocking colors spoke of passion and individual tonal integrity. Or something like that—I'm not exactly what you'd call an art expert. I am, however, an expert at spotting my son's work. The trademark of his artistic brilliance is a simple sticker added to the pictures that he draws and colors. No artistic endeavor is complete without one. It may be a flower, bug, or bear, but that crowning touch is inevitable—"The Sticker."

Quickly I recognized the picture that had to be my son's. In the top left-hand corner of an unidentifiable watercolor creation was a small black-and-red ladybug sticker. "Do you see mine, Daddy?" he asked eagerly.

With the pride of Van Gogh's dad I replied, "Of course I do. What a beautiful sticker!"

With nonchalant confidence my son replied, "I know."

Enhancing the beauty of God's creation is the signature mark of His handiwork, the pride of His creative masterpiece—a man and a woman. They have names, faces, and identities—just as you and I do. Humanity stands out like a vibrant sticker on an already beautiful creation, signaling God's proudest thoughts: *This is Mine, and this is good.* What a creation! What a Creator! Look at the story:

"So God created man in his own image, in the image of God he created him; male and female he created them" (Genesis 1:27).

"This is the written account of Adam's line. When God created man, he made him in the likeness of God. He created them male and female and blessed them. And when they were created, he called them 'man'" (Genesis 5:1, 2).

Why are people such a vital part of creation? The Creator makes man and woman in His image—in His likeness. We are the sticker on His creation. Forget for a moment what we may be like today. Picture God's face (if you can) full of pride when He made Adam and Eve and thought it was *really* good. Who is this God who creates creatures in His image—like Him?

"For he has rescued us from the dominion of darkness and brought us into the kingdom of the Son he loves, in whom we have redemption, the forgiveness of sins. He is the image of the invisible God, the firstborn over all creation. For by him all things were created: things in heaven and on earth, visible and invisible, whether thrones or powers or rulers or authorities; all things were created by him and for him" (Colossians 1:13-16).

Did you see it? Look at another verse:

"In the past God spoke to our forefathers through the prophets at many times and in various ways, but in these last days he has spoken to us by his Son, whom he appointed heir of all things, and through whom he made the universe" (Hebrews 1:1, 2).

The Creator, the one who stamps the world with a picture of Him in the form of humanity, is the Son, Jesus Christ. As wonderful as the reality of God's creative work is, even more so is the reality of His commitment to restore His precious creatures (us) to life, as He becomes one of us.

Life of Christ

John 1:1-14

"In the beginning was the Word, and the Word was with God, and the Word was God. He was with

God in the beginning. Through him all things were made; without him nothing was made that has been made. In him was life, and that life was the light of men. . . . The Word became flesh and made his dwelling among us. We have seen his glory, the glory of the One and Only, who came from the Father, full of grace and truth."

We live in a world that often makes it difficult to see the beauty of the Creator and His creation. Some argue that there is no Creator, that only chance began the existence of life on earth millions of years ago. But those who believe the Bible's account of our beginnings stand in awe of the Creator, asking, "Who is the amazing God who called this world to be by His own breath?"

Open Questions

What do you think it means to be "made in the image of God"? What glimpses of God can you still see in others?

We Believe

Creation

"God is Creator of all things, and has revealed in Scripture the authentic account of His creative activity. In six days the Lord made 'the heaven and the earth' and all living things upon the earth, and rested on the seventh day of that first week. Thus He established the Sabbath as a perpetual memorial of His completed creative work. The first man and woman were made in the image of God as the crowning work of Creation, given dominion over the world, and charged with responsibility to care for it. When the world was finished it was 'very good,' declaring the glory of God."*

    a. Genesis 1

    b. Genesis 2

    c. Exodus 20:8-11

    d. Psalm 19:1-6

    e. Psalm 33:6, 9

    f. Psalm 104

    g. Hebrews 11:3

I Believe

Write your own statement of belief about the glory of Creation. You may choose to focus on the beauty, uniqueness, and meaning of this event, or you may decide to write about your beliefs in light of the current ideas about evolution.

Way to Pray

In your prayers to God this week, converse with Him about the Creation event. You may want to read about it in Genesis 1 and meditate and talk to God about what happened each day of Creation. Ultimately, in light of the wonder of God's creative power, practice praising God this week for His creative ability.

More Than Words

God's creative genius reveals itself in a variety of ways. How can you demonstrate God's glory in the natural world or in the way you personally live your life as the crowning work of Creation? Think of some tangible ways to do this.

Interview: Ask someone:

What place on earth reminds you most of God's creative power and why? What experience or event in your life causes you to think of Creation? Have you ever had a conversation with someone who does not believe in God as the Creator? Describe the conversation and what you talked about.

In the Mirror

Write some of your thoughts down as you reflect on our world's creation, especially God's crowning event of making people. How do we glorify God with our lives today as His sticker on Creation? The first of the three angels' messages in Revelation speaks of worshiping the Creator. Reflect on this passage and write your thoughts and perspective.

Revelation 14:7

"He said in a loud voice, 'Fear God and give him glory, because the hour of his judgment has come. Worship him who made the heavens, the earth, the sea and the springs of water.'"

---

* *Seventh-day Adventists Believe,* p. 68.

The Law of God

I've heard all the jokes, especially in the setting of weddings, about the dreaded "in-laws." In-laws are people you become family to through the act of marrying one of their family members. (That's my personal definition.) So when I married Julie, Julie's mother became my "mother-in-law." While it's not a hard concept to get, I don't like the term *in-law*. While many may have uncomfortable or awkward feelings about their "in-laws," I happen to love my "in-laws" so much that I don't even use the term *law* to describe the relationship. Love describes my relationship to Julie—and her family. I don't love them just because I'm legally attached to them. I'm proud to be associated with them because of who they are as persons. It would stifle the relationship if it were solely a legal association. Two points are important in the in-law relationship: (1) the marriage—obviously vital, and (2) the new family mentality. Now I belong to a bigger group who love the same people I do.

Look at the way Scripture uses the analogy of marriage to describe the way we relate to God:

"As a young man marries a maiden, so will your sons marry you; as a bridegroom rejoices over his bride, so will your God rejoice over you" (Isaiah 62:5).

Love pours out of this analogy. We glimpse how God feels about us, His children. In Jeremiah He recalls the obedience of the children of Israel with the same attitude of deep devotion and marital bliss:

"Go and proclaim in the hearing of Jerusalem: 'I remember the devotion of your youth, how as a bride you loved me and followed me through the desert, through a land not sown'" (Jeremiah 2:2).

As you study the law of God, watch Jesus as He tries to show that the motivation, the basis of the law, is a response of total love and devotion. It's not a list of rules to manage your life, but merely the expression of the way we honor the ones we love. As we approach life in God's family it is not with an attitude of being an "in-law," but one who is "in-love" with the Father.

According to Scripture, "the Law" was more than the Ten Commandments. It was the first five books of Moses, the prophets, the Psalms, the whole Old Testament, as we know it, as well as an oral tradition.

Look at the scene in the passage below and share your insights about how God wants us to relate to the law and how to make it meaningful and practical.

Life of Christ

Matthew 22:34-40

"Hearing that Jesus had silenced the Sadducees, the Pharisees got together. One of them, an expert in the law, tested him with this question: 'Teacher, which is the greatest commandment in the Law?' Jesus replied: '"Love the Lord your God with all your heart and with all your soul and with all your mind." This is the first and greatest commandment. And the second is like it: "Love your neighbor as yourself." All the Law and the Prophets hang on these two commandments.'"

Many people today ignore God's Ten Commandments as outdated rules that really don't apply anymore. As you read the Ten Commandments, ask yourself, "What would this world be like if we shelved the Ten Commandments?" How close do you think we are to that moment? Do you think we will ever get there? If so, what will take the place of God's law?

We Believe

The Law of God

"The great principles of God's law are embodied in the Ten Commandments and exemplified in the life of Christ. They express God's love, will, and purposes concerning human conduct and relationships and are binding upon all people in every age. These precepts are the basis of God's covenant with His people and the standard in God's judgment. Through the agency of the Holy Spirit they point out sin and awaken a sense of need for a Saviour. Salvation is all of grace and not of works, but its fruitage is obedience to the Commandments. This obedience develops Christian character and results in a sense of well-being. It is an evidence of our love for the Lord and our concern for our fellow men. The obedience of faith demonstrates the power of Christ to transform lives, and therefore strengthens Christian witness."* (Chain-reference the following verses and paraphrase them in your own words.)

    a. Exodus 20:1-17

    b. Psalm 40:7, 8

    c. Matthew 22:36-40

    d. Deuteronomy 28:1-14

    e. Matthew 5:17-20

    f. John 15:7-10

    g. 1 John 5:3

    h. Psalm 19:7-14

In your own words, how do you think the law relates to those who are saved by God's grace and enter into His family?

Way to Pray

As you pray, consider how keeping God's law would change your life today. If you were to decide to keep His commandments, what would you need to do? What would you need to stop doing?

Write a prayer to God about the commitments you will have to make with each commandment and how it will make your life better. Each day choose a different commandment to reflect and pray about.

More Than Words

Interview: Invite someone to share a response to the following interview questions:

How do you explain the balance between being saved by God's grace and being obedient to God's law?

How does keeping the Ten Commandments affect the quality of your daily life?

Which commandment do you think would change the world most significantly if everyone were to be convicted of it and start keeping it?

Character Search

Try to get to know someone this week you didn't really know very well before. Ask questions that will get at the heart of who they really are, such as "What do you really enjoy doing?" "What do you want to become?" As you get to know that certain individual, think about how you might begin to know God more fully.

Make a list of some things you want to know about God's character, who He is and what He is like. Read and reflect on Philip's famous plea, "Show us the Father" (John 14:6-10).

In the Mirror

How has this study helped you see God's character more clearly? In what ways does God's law reveal what He is like?

---

* *Seventh-day Adventists Believe*, p. 232.

The Sabbath

Open Questions

Rank in order of importance to you (1—most important, 5—least important)
The Sabbath is primarily about:

___ Serving others in love

___ Resting from physical work

___ Worshiping together with other believers

___ Being with family

___ Stopping normal activities to commune personally with God

Opening Story

It is a well-known fact that students do not all learn the same way. Some learn visually, some through music, and others by active use of their hands. This day turned out to be one of those moments in college classrooms in which everyone learned, especially the teacher.

The class consisted almost exclusively of college freshmen, taking a course on the life and ministry of Christ. As the teacher, I had devised a variety of ways to engage them in an active discovery of gospel themes. Still, I could never—not in a million years—have devised a lesson plan so powerful that every student would leave the room a different person.

It was Veterans Day. Usually I would plan a discussion in which students could say something to affirm the veterans in their life. But I had forgotten entirely about the holiday. What is even more difficult to imagine is that the only student who was not a freshman had served in Vietnam. John's papers, describing some of the horror of war in the jungles—friends killed, villages decimated—thoughtfully wove the beautiful truths of the Savior into his traumatic experience. He shared his overwhelming shock and anger as he returned home, only to be mistreated by the country he had risked his life to protect. How could I have missed it this day?

I realized it in the first few minutes of class. As the students took a quiz, I glanced at the calendar—Veterans Day. By the time they turned in their papers I thought I could salvage the moment. "How many of you knew when you came to class that it was Veterans Day?" I asked. They looked at me with blank stares. John quietly stared at his desk, not wishing to look up.

"That's right; other colleges don't have to come to class today!" one student observed.

Another student chimed in, "I know, this college is constantly robbing us of legitimate days off." The others murmured in agreement, and the air became alive with the hope that I would dismiss class. By now I wanted to crawl under the desk.

"We need a day off."

"I have so much to study for."

"It is a national holiday, right—like Labor Day?"

"We should be camping."

I glanced at John as the students stared at me. His face was red, with either embarrassment or anger—I could not tell. The classroom grew quiet. The gravity of the moment began to dawn on several students as they recalled the first day of class when we had all introduced ourselves. John had mentioned that he was in college on a scholarship from his service in the Marines.

Realizing that I couldn't avoid the tension or dismiss it, I took responsibility for my part in forgetting this day. Apologizing personally to John, I mentioned to the rest of the class that he had served in Vietnam. One thoughtful student on the front row asked him in a quiet voice, "What was it like?"

Never had anyone in my class asked a question that demanded everyone's attention like that one. John, although quite embarrassed, mentioned briefly the more rudimentary details of war in Vietnam—the weather, the people, the terrain, and the conditions. The class was quiet again. "Did you lose any friends in battle?" someone said. The questions and answers continued for the rest of the period. At the end of class everyone gave a spontaneous round of applause for John. Veterans Day had become what it was meant to be.

The Sabbath had lost its beauty and honor for many in the time of Christ. Rules and stipulations hid its intended purpose. Here again we see Jesus seeking to shake people from their unthinking religion and awaken an experience that demonstrates God's grace and His mighty power in the lives of His created beings.

Life of Christ

Luke 13:10-16

"On a Sabbath Jesus was teaching in one of the synagogues, and a woman was there who had been crippled by a spirit for eighteen years. She was bent over and could not straighten up at all. When Jesus saw her, he called her forward and said to her, 'Woman, you are set free from your infirmity.' Then he put his hands on her, and immediately she straightened up and praised God. Indignant because Jesus had healed on the Sabbath, the synagogue ruler said to the people, 'There are six days for work. So come and be healed on those days, not on the Sabbath.' The Lord answered him, 'You hypocrites! Doesn't each of you on the Sabbath untie his ox or donkey from the stall and lead it out to give it water? Then should not this woman, a daughter of Abraham, whom Satan has kept bound for eighteen long years, be set free on the Sabbath day from what bound her?'"

As you study the truth of the seventh-day Sabbath, consider some of the following questions:

What is the purpose of the Sabbath?

How did Jesus model Sabbathkeeping?

How can we honor God by our time on the seventh day of the week?

We Believe

The Sabbath

"The beneficent Creator, after the six days of Creation, rested on the seventh day and instituted the Sabbath for all people as a memorial of Creation. The fourth commandment of God's unchangeable law requires the observance of this seventh-day Sabbath as the day of rest, worship, and ministry in harmony with the teaching and practice of Jesus, the Lord of the Sabbath. The Sabbath is a day of delightful communion with God and one another. It is a symbol of our redemption in Christ, a sign of our sanctification, a token of our allegiance, and a foretaste of our eternal future in God's kingdom. The Sabbath is God's perpetual sign of His eternal covenant between Him and His people. Joyful observance of this holy time from evening to evening, sunset to sunset, is a celebration of God's creative and redemptive acts."* (Chain-reference these verses in your Bible and be sure to mark or write notes about them that have particular meaning or raise questions you would like to talk about.)

a. Genesis 2:1-3
b. Exodus 20:8-11
c. Deuteronomy 5:12-15
d. Exodus 31:13-17
e. Luke 4:16
f. Ezekiel 20:12, 20
g. Matthew 12:1-12
h. Isaiah 58:13, 14
i. Isaiah 56:5, 6

Way to Pray

Talk to God about what you really love about the Sabbath day as well as what frustrates or confuses you.

More Than Words

Interview: Invite someone to share with you their perspective on the Sabbath experience. Ask them: Describe the most meaningful Sabbath you have ever had.

What is the main reason you keep the Sabbath? How does it shape your relationship with God?

On what principles or criteria do you make choices about what to do on the Sabbath day?

As you finish this study, you may want to look at the passages from the life of Christ and plan your next Sabbath after the pattern of how He kept it. Do it with other believers who have the same desire to remember who God is and why He wants us to pause to remember His creation. (Write out the things you want to do and share them with your partner and friends.)

In the Mirror

Reflect on the following statement: "Keeping the Bible Sabbath can be an invasion into your life." How does the Sabbath intrude on our way of living?

Reflect on how the Sabbath can reorient your priorities, relationships, and spiritual experience.

What is going to change about your life now that you understand the purpose of Sabbath and the joy that awaits you?

* *Seventh-day Adventists Believe,* p. 248.

The Life, Death, and Resurrection of Christ

Opening Story

"During hard times in the darkness of winter in an Alaskan Eskimo village a young man of unequaled courage might go out into the bitter cold in search of food for his people. Armed only with a pointed stick and his compassion for his starving village, he would wander, anticipating the attack of a polar bear. Having no natural fear of humans, a polar bear will stalk and eat a man. In the attack the Eskimo hunter would wave his hands and spear to anger the bear and make him rise up on his hind legs to over ten feet in height; and then, with the spear braced on his foot, the hunter would aim for the heart as the weight of the bear came down upon his spear. With the heart pierced, the bear might live long enough to maim or kill this noble hunter. Loving family and friends would then follow his tracks out of the village and find food for their survival and evidence of profound courage."[1]

The illustration wonderfully describes courage, commitment to family and friends, and willingness to lay down one's life for loved ones. But such analogies have problems.

One involves the fact that the bold hunter risks his life for the survival of his loved ones. The problem? I know a lot of godless people who would risk their lives for their family, especially their children. No question—I would. If it came down to me or my sandy-haired boy with that disarming grin, I'd give my life for him. I'm certain that even those who claim to be skeptics or atheists would as well. The

Eskimo does what anyone would do for the ones they love. Wouldn't you? The difference is that Christ faced the bear (so to speak) for everyone—anyone. Whether they returned His love or not. Romans 5:8 says that "while we were still sinners, Christ died for us." That is, while we were His enemies: hateful, rebellious, indifferent, ungrateful, inconsistent, unpopular, psychotic, sexually perverted, insane, undeserving. The truth is that while I would unquestioningly lay down my life for my son, I doubt I would die for my enemy. But Jesus did.

The other problem raised in this illustration is the notion that the brave Eskimo may or may not live. There was a chance he would survive, perhaps with a few scars or even the loss of a limb. We take risks all the time. But when Christ became a baby, He became destined for death—death on a cross. He had no other choice, no other way that He could save you and me. In Gethsemane it was clear to Jesus that the Father's will was the way of the cross. He would, in fact, experience an ugly separation from His Father. The Holy God would regard Him as sinful so that you and I might be "the righteousness of God." It was a sure thing. He would die. And it would be terrible.

One final problem concerns those in the igloo—that's us. You and I would follow the footsteps of the brave Eskimo into the unknown because it might mean our survival. Unfortunately, many stay in the igloo and never make the journey to Calvary to receive the saving grace that comes from the sacrificed Son. We think we can survive the winter on our own. It's too cold out there to leave the igloo. We don't have the right shoes or are too busy decorating the inside of the igloo. It's crazy, I know. But that's who we are.

C. S. Lewis made an interesting point when he wrote, "A man who was merely a man and said the sort of things Jesus said wouldn't be a great moral teacher. He'd either be a lunatic—on the level with a man who says he's a poached egg—or else he'd be the devil of hell. You must make your choice. Either this man was, and is, the Son of God, or else a madman or something worse." [2]

Only rarely did Jesus ever mention why He came. But in each conversation we catch a glimpse of God's purpose in sending His Son into the world. Notice what He said about Himself and reflect on each statement as to what His mission means to you as you surrender all of yourself to Him.

Life of Christ

Matthew 9:11-13

"When the Pharisees saw this, they asked his disciples, 'Why does your teacher eat with tax collectors and "sinners"?' On hearing this, Jesus said, 'It is not the healthy who need a doctor, but the sick. But go and learn what this means: "I desire mercy, not sacrifice." For I have not come to call the righteous, but sinners.'"

Matthew 20:20-28

"Then the mother of Zebedee's sons came to Jesus with her sons and, kneeling down, asked a favor of him. 'What is it you want?' he asked. She said, 'Grant that one of these two sons of mine may sit at your right and the other at your left in your kingdom.' 'You don't know what you are asking,' Jesus said to them. 'Can you drink the cup I am going to drink?' 'We can,' they answered. Jesus said to them, 'You will indeed drink from my cup, but to sit at my right or left is not for me to grant. These places belong to those for whom they have been prepared by my Father.' When the ten heard about this, they were indignant with the two brothers. Jesus called them together and said, 'You know that the rulers of the Gentiles lord it over them, and their high officials exercise authority over them. Not so with you. Instead, whoever wants to become great among you must be your servant, and whoever wants to be first must be your slave—just as the Son of Man did not come to be served, but to serve, and to give his life as a ransom for many.'"

Luke 19:5-10

"When Jesus reached the spot, he looked up and said to him, 'Zacchaeus, come down immediately. I must stay at your house today.' So he came down at once and welcomed him gladly. All the people saw this and began to mutter, 'He has gone to be the guest of a "sinner."' But Zacchaeus stood up and said to the Lord, 'Look, Lord! Here and now I give half of my possessions to the poor, and if I have cheated anybody out of anything, I will pay back four times the amount.' Jesus said to him,

'Today salvation has come to this house, because this man, too, is a son of Abraham. For the Son of Man came to seek and to save what was lost.'"

Matthew 5:17, 18

"Do not think that I have come to abolish the Law or the Prophets; I have not come to abolish them but to fulfill them. I tell you the truth, until heaven and earth disappear, not the smallest letter, not the least stroke of a pen, will by any means disappear from the Law until everything is accomplished."

We Believe

The Life, Death, and Resurrection of Christ

"In Christ's life of perfect obedience to God's will, His suffering, death, and resurrection, God provided the only means of atonement for human sin, so that those who by faith accept this atonement may have eternal life, and the whole creation may better understand the infinite and holy love of the Creator. This perfect atonement vindicates the righteousness of God's law and the graciousness of His character; for it both condemns our sin and provides for our forgiveness. The death of Christ is substitutionary and expiatory, reconciling and transforming. The resurrection of Christ proclaims God's triumph over the forces of evil, and for those who accept the atonement assures their final victory over sin and death. It declares the Lordship of Jesus Christ, before whom every knee in heaven and on earth will bow."[3]

(Chain-reference the following passages in your Bible and comment on what each says to you about where you are at in your life today.)

   a. John 3:16

   b. Isaiah 53

   c. 1 Peter 2:21, 22

d. 1 John 2:2; 4:10

e. Colossians 2:15

f. Philippians 2:6-11

Way to Pray

Imagine the final moments of Christ's life on Calvary. As you picture the scene, hear the voices, feel the hatred in the air. After you meditate on the cross, say to God whatever you feel you need to tell Him. If God were to speak to you in the light of Calvary, what do you think He would say about your life right now?

More Than Words

Interview: Ask someone you know to be spiritually thoughtful to respond to the following interview questions:

If you had only three stories or events to share from the life of Christ, which ones would you choose and why?

What do you think is the most important saying in the four Gospels?

Share an experience, story, or event from your life during which the life of Christ was especially meaningful to you. (Give them time for this question.)

In the Bible we find essential stories and sayings that make the message of Scripture real and life-changing for us. What moments in your life (choose three) have been pivotal?

In the Mirror

How has the study of the life and mission of Jesus been helpful to you? What do you wish you knew more about?

[1] James S. Hewett, *Illustrations Unlimited,* pp. 68, 69.
[2] C. S. Lewis, *Mere Christianity,* pp. 40, 41.
[3] *Seventh-day Adventists Believe,* p. 106.

The Lord's Supper

Opening Story

The collision was unavoidable. I was hurtling around a blind turn, and Karen, heading right toward me, was neither looking for nor expecting me to come racing around the corner. We were short of deacons on this particular Sabbath, so I was sprinting around the outside of the church, hands tightly gripping the silver tray of small grape juice goblets and thumb-sized pieces of bread I held in front of me. Even as we ran into each other I was thinking, *I hope nobody comes around this corner because if they'd . . . Crash!* Grape juice went everywhere as the toothpaste-cap-sized goblets tumbled to the ground. Karen had spatters of grape juice on her plain yellow dress. I was the last person she wanted to, or had expected to, run into—literally.

"I'm sorry!" she cried. "I guess you are wondering why I'm leaving."

"Well, actually, I'm just kind of wet right now, so I hadn't had much time to think about where you were headed. Are you leaving because it's Communion Sabbath?" (If she was, boy, I'd have given it to her.)

She nodded. "I didn't know it was today, and lately . . . I just . . . well . . . I just don't think I should take Communion right now."

I picked up the goblets and the bread and put them back in the tray. "Would you mind telling why you feel as though you shouldn't participate?"

She looked away. "I just haven't been very close to God lately, and I don't think I deserve to do this."

I thought about what she said for a moment. "Karen, I want you to know that when you are far away from God is when you are most ready for Communion. Communion is not for those who are ready; it is for those who are aware of their sinfulness and want to remember God's work of grace on Calvary for them. When you feel far away is when you need this the most. We all forget the significance of Christ's sacrifice, so we do this to remember, not to show how ready we are.

"Plus, if you don't participate in the Communion service, your pastor will chase you down and baptize you in grape juice until you straighten up!" I said with a crooked smile. She looked up and laughed. We walked back into the church, and she sat down while I went to the kitchen to get more juice.

During the testimony time in the little church Karen stood and told the congregation about her collision. "I felt like staying away. I think that what Satan wants more than anything else is to get us to leave when God's hope is that we draw closer."

The incident reminded all of us that day of God's amazing grace. "Do this to remember Me," Jesus said. "Remember Me." Sometimes we remain away from moments of remembrance because it is awkward. Other times our hesitation involves our strong awareness of sin. You couldn't run into (except perhaps in Karen's case) a better opportunity to receive grace. Communion is really only for those who know they need it.

What do you use to remind yourself of important things in your life? A list? A string around your index finger? In our fast-paced world it is so easy to forget even the most significant things. God intended the Lord's Supper to be an active reminder (much as the Sabbath is a reminder of God as our Creator) that Christ is our Redeemer and Lord. Read the following verses and notice how this supper is more than just a "last meal."

Life of Christ

Mark 14:17-26

"When evening came, Jesus arrived with the Twelve. While they were reclining at the table eating, he said, 'I tell you the truth, one of you will betray me—one who is eating with me.' They were saddened, and one by one they said to him, 'Surely not I?' 'It is one of the Twelve,' he replied, 'one who dips bread into the bowl with me. The Son of Man will go just as it is written about him. But woe to that man who betrays the Son of Man! It would be better for him if he had not been born.' While they were eating, Jesus took bread, gave thanks and broke it, and gave it to his disciples, saying, 'Take it; this is my body.' Then he took the cup, gave thanks and offered it to them, and they all drank from it. 'This is my blood of the covenant, which is poured out for many,' he said to them. 'I tell you the truth, I will not drink again of the fruit of the vine until that day when I drink it anew in the kingdom of God.' When they had sung a hymn, they went out to the Mount of Olives."

Luke 24:30, 31

"When he was at the table with them, he took bread, gave thanks, broke it and began to give it to them. Then their eyes were opened and they recognized him, and he disappeared from their sight."

We Believe

The Lord's Supper

"The Lord's Supper is a participation in the emblems of the body and blood of Jesus as an expression of faith in Him, our Lord and Saviour. In this experience of Communion Christ is present to meet and strengthen His people. As we partake, we joyfully proclaim the Lord's death until He comes again. Preparation for the Supper includes self-examination, repentance, and confession. The Master ordained the service of foot washing to signify renewed cleansing, to express a willingness to serve one another in Christlike humility, and to unite our hearts in love. The Communion service is open to all believing Christians."*

    a. 1 Corinthians 10:16, 17; 11:23-30
    b. Matthew 26:17-30

c. Revelation 3:20

d. John 6:48-63

e. John 13:1-17

Way to Pray

Write a prayer to God focusing on what you remember most about Calvary and the sacrifice Christ paid for you there. Invite God to remind you in other ways about your relationship with Him.

More Than Words

Have a Communion service or participate in a memorial supper for the Lord's death. Do this with friends or your partner in this study. Reflect on the moments of Calvary and then plan the event.

Interview: Invite someone to share with you their responses to the following questions:

Share with me your most memorable Communion service. Why was it so special?

How can a person experience the real significance of the Communion service and make it as meaningful as possible?

How is foot washing an important part of the Communion experience?

In the Mirror

Reflect on the parts of your relationship with God that you tend to forget about and write about some ideas you might have to remember God's work of grace in your life.

* *Seventh-day Adventists Believe,* p. 194.

Spiritual Gifts

Every time I make a major purchase I do two things: (1) buy an extended service warranty and (2) pray. I pray because if whatever I buy breaks, I don't have a mechanical bone in my body to fix it. I remember working with my dad on the car. When he asked me to hand him a Phillips screwdriver, I left the garage and made my way to Phillip's house (he lived about six houses down) to borrow his screwdriver. I had no idea why his was so special, but I just did what my father requested. Returning with Phillip's screwdriver, I handed it to my dad. "Here you go," I announced proudly.

"Where have you been?" he said as he popped his head out from under the car.

"Getting Phillip's screwdriver for you!" With a smile he then proceeded to show me the difference between a Phillips screwdriver and a regular one. While I now know the difference between a Phillips screwdriver and Phillip's screwdriver, I'm still not good at using either.

Some people are wired for certain tasks. God created us with different abilities. Some we learn and develop over time, while others are inherent in our makeup. I can force myself to learn music and play an instrument, but true musicians have music in their makeup. They are passionate about it. Whether you learn a skill or whether you are born with it, the fact remains that God needs you and your abilities. When you surrender yourself to God, you also surrender all of your abilities for the purpose of the mission of the body of Christ.

"Therefore, I urge you, brothers, in view of God's mercy, to offer your bodies as living sacrifices, holy and pleasing to God—this is your spiritual act of worship" (Romans 12:1).

This is what it means to worship God. It is not sitting in church quietly for an hour or two once a week. Worshiping God is giving all of yourself to Him. Look at how Jesus turned His disciples loose to do the work of service for God.

Life of Christ

Luke 10:1-20

"After this the Lord appointed seventy-two others and sent them two by two ahead of him to every town and place where he was about to go. He told them, 'The harvest is plentiful, but the workers are few. Ask the Lord of the harvest, therefore, to send out workers into his harvest field. Go! I am sending you out like lambs among wolves. Do not take a purse or bag or sandals; and do not greet anyone on the road. When you enter a house, first say, "Peace to this house." If a man of peace is there, your peace will rest on him; if not, it will return to you. Stay in that house, eating and drinking whatever they give you, for the worker deserves his wages. Do not move around from house to house. When you enter a town and are welcomed, eat what is set before you. Heal the sick who are there and tell them, "The kingdom of God is near you." But when you enter a town and are not welcomed, go into its streets and say, "Even the dust of your town that sticks to our feet we wipe off against you. Yet be sure of this: The kingdom of God is near." I tell you, it will be more bearable on that day for Sodom than for that town. Woe to you, Korazin! Woe to you, Bethsaida! For if the miracles that were performed in you had been performed in Tyre and Sidon, they would have repented long ago, sitting in sackcloth and ashes. But it will be more bearable for Tyre and Sidon at the judgment than for you. And you, Capernaum, will you be lifted up to the skies? No, you will go down to the depths. He who listens to you listens to me; he who rejects you rejects me; but he who rejects me rejects him who sent me.' The seventy-two returned with joy and said, 'Lord, even the demons submit to us in your name.' He replied, 'I saw Satan fall like lightning from heaven. I have given you authority to trample on snakes and scorpions and to overcome all the power of the enemy; nothing will harm you. However, do not rejoice that the spirits submit to you, but rejoice that your names are written in heaven.' "

Christ sent each disciple. I don't know how He paired them up. I'm not sure who went to what place. But Jesus empowered them to work. Each had a role to play. It's the same with us. Every believer has received a gift—a spiritual gift—to use for the purpose of building the kingdom of God on earth. Some have a few gifts, others have many, but each gift is valuable, and the church needs all the gifts if its mission is to succeed.

What is a spiritual gift?

When or how is it given?

How do I discover what God wants me to do?

We Believe

Spiritual Gifts

"God bestows upon all members of His church in every age spiritual gifts which each member is to employ in loving ministry for the common good of the church and of humanity. Given by the agency of the Holy Spirit, who apportions to each member as He wills, the gifts provide all abilities and ministries needed by the church to fulfill its divinely ordained functions. According to the Scriptures, these gifts include such ministries as faith, healing, prophecy, proclamation, teaching, administration, reconciliation, compassion, and self-sacrificing service and charity for the help and encouragement of people. Some members are called of God and endowed by the Spirit for functions recognized by the church in pastoral, evangelistic, apostolic, and teaching ministries particularly needed to equip the members for service, to build up the church to spiritual maturity, and to foster unity of the faith and knowledge of God. When members employ these spiritual gifts as faithful stewards of God's varied grace, the church is protected from the destructive influence of false doctrine, grows with a growth that is from God, and is built up in faith and love."*

    a. Romans 12:4-8

    b. 1 Corinthians 12:9-11, 27, 28

    c. Ephesians 4:8, 11-16

    d. Acts 6:1-7

    e. 1 Timothy 3:1-13

    f. 1 Peter 4:10, 11

Take the spiritual gifts questionnaire (see Appendix A) and see what you think your gifts are. Compare your findings with your partner or your group and talk about how you feel about them.

Way to Pray

Prayer Focus This Week

Thank God for the specific gifts you think He has given you. Mention them by name, and ask God to affirm them in your life. (He can do that only when you start actively doing those tasks and ministries.)

More Than Words

Since God intended spiritual gifts to build up the body of Christ (the church), write a letter to your pastor and/or church board describing what you think your gifts are, and ask them to involve you in or enable you to work for the ministry of the church—or, to use the old baseball adage, "Where do you want me to play?"

For your spiritual gift, think of several specific tasks that you can do that develop your gift(s) and begin to reflect on and share what is happening to you as you become what God designed you to be.

In the Mirror

Reflect on your experiences with spiritual gifts this week. What do you hope will happen with your service to God during the next few months? What hopes do you have about how this will help you become more like Christ?

---

* *Seventh-day Adventists Believe*, p. 206.

The Church as the Body of Christ

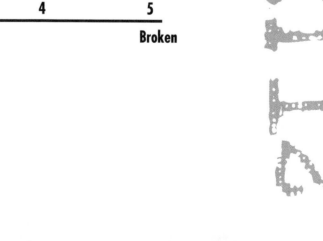

Open Questions

Either/Or

Is the primary purpose of the church to provide a place for believers to grow *or* to focus on reaching unbelievers?

Show where you think your church is at on the continuum below.
1—Lively, strong, and effective
5—Broken and divided, with only a few parts working

1	2	3	4	5
Alive				**Broken**

Why do you think your church is this way?

Opening Story

Outside of recess and PE, lunchtime has few competing highlights during the school day. One day I visited my wife while she worked on developing a remedial program for students, and thus I found myself spending lunchtime in the first grade. I enjoyed watching the students rustle around the classroom with their lunch pails and small cartons of milk. One boy with bright-red curly hair, however, remained in his seat. My heart sank into my stomach as someone announced out loud what was obvious to anyone watching, "Billy doesn't have a lunch."

At first I thought the remark was cruel. But before I could react the roomful of students scurried into action. What I saw permanently engraved the most beautiful image of community into my mind. Each student began breaking off pieces of their peanut-butter-and-jelly sandwiches and placed them on a tray that they passed around the room. I never saw who started the tray around. Bags of chips popped open and littered the brown plastic cafeteria tray with samples of every flavor known to first graders across the land, plus half of a banana, tons of carrot and celery sticks, and a bounty of cookies broken in half. As someone set the tray filled with food before the hungry lad, a grin crept shyly across his sweet freckled face.

Embarrassed? A little. Tickled to death at the feast fit for five first graders looming before him like a small mountain? No question.

Actually, I had many questions. Who started the tray? When did they learn to do this? Why didn't *I* forget *my* lunch? "Where did they learn to do this?" I asked the teacher. He smiled. "It happened a few years back when one of my students would share his lunch with anyone who forgot theirs. Everyone joined in, and then it just became kind of an unspoken rule in the classroom. When someone forgets a lunch, everyone helps." The simple way the kids created community in their classroom stunned me.

Two truths strike me as I remember that day in the classroom. 1. When everyone gives, what is given is so abundant that it leaves those who are helped with a powerful experience of God's overflowing grace. 2. The revolution of "the big lunch" started with one child.

Jesus began the church when one person finally understood the purpose. What did He really mean? Was Peter the newly appointed church leader? Is Jesus talking about Himself as the rock?

I think it is safe to say that Peter had a long way to go. It is also safe to say that entrance into the church does not go through Peter. Jesus simply says, "I'm going to start with you."

The church—is it a building? an organization? The various symbols Scripture uses to describe the church are powerful windows for seeing what God is like and how He created us as people who thrive in community. Look at the following biblical story and see what you think.

Life of Christ

Matthew 16:13-18

"When Jesus came to the region of Caesarea Philippi, he asked his disciples, 'Who do people say the Son of Man is?' They replied, 'Some say John the Baptist; others say Elijah; and still others, Jeremiah or one of the prophets.' 'But what about you?' he asked. 'Who do you say I am?' Simon Peter answered, 'You are the Christ, the Son of the living God.' Jesus replied, 'Blessed are you, Simon son of Jonah, for this was not revealed to you by man, but by my Father in heaven. And I tell you that you are Peter, and on this rock I will build my church, and the gates of Hades will not overcome it.'"

We Believe

The Church as the Body of Christ

"The church is the community of believers who confess Jesus Christ as Lord and Saviour. In continuity with the people of God in Old Testament times, we are called out from the world; and we join together for worship, for fellowship, for instruction in the Word, for the celebration of the Lord's

Supper, for service to all mankind, and for the worldwide proclamation of the gospel. The church derives its authority from Christ, who is the incarnate Word, and from the Scriptures, which are the written Word. The church is God's family; adopted by Him as children, its members live on the basis of the new covenant. The church is the body of Christ, a community of faith of which Christ Himself is the Head. The church is the bride for whom Christ died that He might sanctify and cleanse her. At His return in triumph, He will present her to Himself a glorious church, the faithful of all the ages, the purchase of His blood, not having spot or wrinkle, but holy and without blemish."*

 a. Genesis 12:3
 b. Acts 7:38
 c. Ephesians 4:11-15; 3:8-11
 d. Matthew 28:19, 20
 e. Matthew 16:13-20; 18:17, 18
 f. Ephesians 1:22, 23; 2:19-22; 5:23-27
 g. Colossians 1:17, 18

What should the church be for its members and for the world around them?

How do you balance personal shortcomings with the powerful impact believers have when they come together to work for God?

Why is the church so important for spreading the gospel to the world?

Way to Pray

A vast difference exists between a gladiator and a spectator. One is active in the fight; the other simply watches. The churches in America desperately need gladiators, not spectators. Talk to God about the problem and invite God to speak to you personally about how you can change your local congregation. Ask Him about the mission He has for you.

More Than Words

Obtain a Seventh-day Adventist yearbook, flip through the pages, and read the names, places, and ministries that comprise the worldwide church. While each local church is a unit, at the same time we are all connected worldwide to others when we worship, believe, and work for the same cause. Take the yearbook and a globe, look up some of the places mentioned in the yearbook, and pray specifically for the mission of the church in an area you feel led to pray for. You may want to write a letter and ask the local leaders how things are going and what you can be praying for as you think of them.

In the Mirror

Reflect on the impact of a congregation on your life. What are some qualities you bring to it?

How do you see your role as a member of Christ's body? How do you see your gifts contributing to the whole?

* *Seventh-day Adventists Believe,* p. 134.

Death and Resurrection

LESSON 5

Opening Story

"A boy and his father were traveling in a car when a bee flew in the open window. The boy was so highly allergic to beestings that both he and his father knew that his life was in danger. As the boy frantically jumped around and tried to avoid the agitated bee, the father calmly reached out and grabbed the bee. When he opened his hands, the bee began to fly again, terrorizing the boy once more. The father then said, 'Look, son,' holding up a hand with an implanted stinger, 'his stinger is gone; he can't hurt you any longer.'"[1]

The experience is the same for those who trust in Christ—the sting of death cannot hurt us. As we study the human condition in death we begin with a story in which Jesus finds Himself in the middle of the most heart-wrenching human scenario: the death of a loved one. As a matter of fact, three stories in the life of Christ describe God's reaction to death. Death is the result of sin, and sin is the enemy of the Savior. Read the three stories and discuss what each one tells you about the power of death.

Life of Christ

John 11:1-44

"Now a man named Lazarus was sick. He was from Bethany, the village of Mary and her sister Martha. This Mary, whose brother Lazarus now lay sick, was the same one who poured perfume on the Lord and wiped his feet with her hair. So the sisters sent word to Jesus, 'Lord, the one you love is sick.' When he heard this, Jesus said, 'This sickness will not end in death. No, it is for God's glory so that God's Son may be glorified through it.' Jesus loved Martha and her sister and Lazarus. Yet when he heard that Lazarus was sick, he stayed where he was two more days. Then he said to his disciples, 'Let us go back to Judea.' 'But Rabbi,' they said, 'a short while ago the Jews tried to stone you, and yet you are going back there?' Jesus answered, 'Are there not twelve hours of daylight? A man who walks by day will not stumble, for he sees by this world's light. It is when he walks by night that he stumbles, for he has no light.' After he had said this, he went on to tell them, 'Our friend Lazarus has fallen asleep; but I am going there to wake him up.' His disciples replied, 'Lord, if he sleeps, he will get better.' Jesus had been speaking of his death, but his disciples thought he meant natural sleep. So then he told them plainly, 'Lazarus is dead, and for your sake I am glad I was not there, so that you may believe. But let us go to him.' Then Thomas (called Didymus) said to the rest of the disciples, 'Let us also go, that we may die with him.' On his arrival, Jesus found that Lazarus had already been in the tomb for four days. Bethany was less than two miles from Jerusalem, and many Jews had come to Martha and Mary to comfort them in the loss of their brother. When Martha heard that Jesus was coming, she went out to meet him, but Mary stayed at home. 'Lord,' Martha said to Jesus, 'if you had been here, my brother would not have died. But I know that even now God will give you whatever you ask.' Jesus said to her, 'Your brother will rise again.' Martha answered, 'I know he will rise again in the resurrection at the last day.' Jesus said to her, 'I am the resurrection and the life. He who believes in me will live, even though he dies; and whoever lives and believes in me will never die. Do you believe this?' 'Yes, Lord,' she told him, 'I believe that you are the Christ, the Son of

God, who was to come into the world.' And after she had said this, she went back and called her sister Mary aside. 'The Teacher is here,' she said, 'and is asking for you.' When Mary heard this, she got up quickly and went to him. Now Jesus had not yet entered the village, but was still at the place where Martha had met him. When the Jews who had been with Mary in the house, comforting her, noticed how quickly she got up and went out, they followed her, supposing she was going to the tomb to mourn there. When Mary reached the place where Jesus was and saw him, she fell at his feet and said, 'Lord, if you had been here, my brother would not have died.' When Jesus saw her weeping, and the Jews who had come along with her also weeping, he was deeply moved in spirit and troubled. 'Where have you laid him?' he asked. 'Come and see, Lord,' they replied. Jesus wept. Then the Jews said, 'See how he loved him!' But some of them said, 'Could not he who opened the eyes of the blind man have kept this man from dying?' Jesus, once more deeply moved, came to the tomb. It was a cave with a stone laid across the entrance. 'Take away the stone,' he said. 'But, Lord,' said Martha, the sister of the dead man, 'by this time there is a bad odor, for he has been there four days.' Then Jesus said, 'Did I not tell you that if you believed, you would see the glory of God?' So they took away the stone. Then Jesus looked up and said, 'Father, I thank you that you have heard me. I knew that you always hear me, but I said this for the benefit of the people standing here, that they may believe that you sent me.' When he had said this, Jesus called in a loud voice, 'Lazarus, come out!' The dead man came out, his hands and feet wrapped with strips of linen, and a cloth around his face. Jesus said to them, 'Take off the grave clothes and let him go.'"

Mark 5:35-43

"While Jesus was still speaking, some men came from the house of Jairus, the synagogue ruler. 'Your daughter is dead,' they said. 'Why bother the teacher any more?' Ignoring what they said, Jesus told the synagogue ruler, 'Don't be afraid; just believe.' He did not let anyone follow him except Peter, James and John the brother of James. When they came to the home of the synagogue ruler, Jesus saw a commotion, with people crying and wailing loudly. He went in and said to them, 'Why all this commotion and wailing? The child is not dead but asleep.' But they laughed at him. After he put them all out, he took the child's father and mother and the disciples who were with him, and went in where the child was. He took her by the hand and said to her, *'Talitha koum!'* (which means, 'Little girl, I say to you, get up!'). Immediately the girl stood up and walked around (she was twelve years old). At this they were completely astonished. He gave strict orders not to let anyone know about this, and told them to give her something to eat."

Luke 7:11-17

"Soon afterward, Jesus went to a town called Nain, and his disciples and a large crowd went along with him. As he approached the town gate, a dead person was being carried out—the only son of his mother, and she was a widow. And a large crowd from the town was with her. When the Lord saw her, his heart went out to her and he said, 'Don't cry.' Then he went up and touched the coffin, and those carrying it stood still. He said, 'Young man, I say to you, get up!' The dead man sat up and began to talk, and Jesus gave him back to his mother. They were all filled with awe and praised God. 'A great prophet has appeared among us,' they said. 'God has come to help his people.' This news about Jesus spread throughout Judea and the surrounding country."

As you look at the preceding stories, what questions or thoughts come to mind? How does our view of death affect the way that we live? What do your friends and family think and believe about death and the resurrection?

We Believe

Death and Resurrection

"The wages of sin is death. But God, who alone is immortal, will grant eternal life to His redeemed. Until that day death is an unconscious state for all people. When Christ, who is our life, appears, the resurrected righteous and the living righteous will be glorified and caught up to meet their Lord. The second resurrection, the resurrection of the unrighteous, will take place a thousand years later." [2]

    a. Romans 6:23

    b. 1 Timothy 6:15, 16

    c. Ecclesiastes 9:5, 6

    d. Psalm 146:3, 4

    e. John 11:11-14

    f. Colossians 3:4

    g. 1 Corinthians 15:51-54

    h. 1 Thessalonians 4:13-17

    i. John 5:28, 29

    j. Revelation 20:1-10

Which passages speak the most to you about God's promise about the hereafter?

Way to Pray

Which passages of Scripture most help you deal with the prospect of death? In your prayers to God, talk openly to Him about your life, your future, and the resurrection day.

More Than Words

Interview: Find someone who has lost a loved one in the past year or so and ask them to share with you what passages or stories from Scripture have brought them the most comfort. Ask them: How does your view of death and resurrection affect the way you live each day?

In the Mirror

Think about what you would want people to say about you at your funeral. Not to be morbid, but what do you want your funeral to be like and why? How does what we know about death and the resurrection help us live in a world in which people die?

---

[1] Michael Green, *1500 Illustrations for Biblical Preaching*, p. 96.
[2] *Seventh-day Adventists Believe*, p. 348.

The Second Coming

One night I was eating dinner with one of my classmates in high school and we were talking about the second coming of Christ. As a teenager I had many questions about this topic. And so did Joey. "We do not have all the answers," his father said, "but we do have all we need to know. The best way to prepare for the Second Coming is simply to live each day as if it were your last."

"I tried that once," Joey told him, "and you grounded me for a month."

Obviously, the answer, "Just live each day as if it were your last," rarely works for us today and probably didn't work any better for the disciples when Jesus mentioned the fact that He would leave—and then come back again.

"There is a story about a man in a large city who was on his way to an interview for a new job with a highly successful company. Well groomed, wearing a nice suit smelling of expensive cologne, the man made his way to the corporate headquarters. As he was waiting for the elevator, an elderly janitor walked by, slipped on the wet floor, and fell down awkwardly. The young man chuckled to himself at the Three Stooges-like humor, unconcerned that the older man might have been hurt. He actually stepped over the fallen janitor, boarded the elevator, went up to the twenty-ninth floor, and entered the reception area of the firm. Soon his name was called, and he was ushered into a beautiful executive office. He was greeted by the woman that was going to conduct the interview. She was the company president.

Immediately, she said, 'By the way, on your way up to see me, did you see anyone who needed help?' 'Yes,' he replied, 'an elderly janitor fell down right in front of me as I was waiting for the elevator.' 'Did you stop to help him?' she asked. 'Well, no, because I believe in promptness, and I didn't want to be late for this very important interview.' 'Of course,' said the company president, 'but you see, that was the interview!'"[1]

Life of Christ

John 14:1-20

" 'Do not let your hearts be troubled. Trust in God; trust also in me. In my Father's house are many rooms; if it were not so, I would have told you. I am going there to prepare a place for you. And if I go and prepare a place for you, I will come back and take you to be with me that you also may be where I am. You know the way to the place where I am going.' Thomas said to him, 'Lord, we don't know where you are going, so how can we know the way?' Jesus answered, 'I am the way and the truth and the life. No one comes to the Father except through me. If you really knew me, you would know my Father as well. From now on, you do know him and have seen him.' Philip said, 'Lord, show us the Father and that will be enough for us.' Jesus answered: 'Don't you know me, Philip, even after I have been among you such a long time? Anyone who has seen me has seen the Father. How can you say, "Show us the Father"? Don't you believe that I am in the Father, and that the Father is in me? The words I say to you are not just my own. Rather, it is the Father, living in me, who is doing his work. Believe me when I say that I am in the Father and the Father is in me; or at least believe on the evidence of the miracles themselves. I tell you the truth, anyone who has faith in me will do what I have been doing. He will do even greater things than these, because I am going to the Father. And I will do whatever you ask in my name, so that the Son may bring glory to the Father. You may ask me for anything in my name, and I will do it. If you love me, you will obey what I command. And I will ask the Father, and he will give you another Counselor to be with you forever—the Spirit of truth. The world cannot accept him, because it neither sees him nor knows him. But you know him, for he lives with you and will be in you. I will not leave you as orphans; I will come to you. Before long, the world will not see me anymore, but you will see me. Because I live, you also will live. On that day you will realize that I am in my Father, and you are in me, and I am in you.'"

What do you wonder about the second coming of Jesus? Make a short list of the big questions you have personally and the kind of answers you hope to glean from this study.

We Believe

The Second Coming

"The second coming of Christ is the blessed hope of the church, the grand climax of the gospel. The Saviour's coming will be literal, personal, visible, and worldwide. When He returns, the righteous dead will be resurrected, and together with the righteous living will be glorified and taken to heaven, but the unrighteous will die. The almost complete fulfillment of most lines of prophecy, together with the present condition of the world, indicates that Christ's coming is imminent. The time of that event has not been revealed, and we are therefore exhorted to be ready at all times."[2]

    a. Revelation 1:7

    b. Matthew 24:43, 44

    c. 1 Thessalonians 4:13-18

    d. 1 Corinthians 15:51-54

e. 2 Thessalonians 1:7-10; 2:8

f. Revelation 14:14-20

g. Revelation 19:11-21

h. Matthew 24

i. 2 Timothy 3:1-5

j. 1 Thessalonians 5:1-6

Way to Pray

Write a prayer to God about your expectations of His soon return. Think about the attitudes you want to foster in your own heart about "the end."

More Than Words

Choose a day during the coming week to practice living as though Jesus would arrive that day. What things do you think you will spend your time doing? What interruptions will you allow to change your schedule? Go about your daily tasks as though Jesus might appear any moment while also realizing what He has called you to do and be. (In other words—you can't skip school, work, the dentist, etc. . . . .) Partner up with a friend and seek to live with an attitude of expectation.

In the Mirror

Describe in detail the coming of Christ as you see it in your imagination. Include the sounds, the smells, the scenes, and describe how you perceive Jesus and His face as He arrives.

[1] James W. Moore, *When You're a Christian, the Whole World Is From Missouri,* p. 139.
[2] *Seventh-day Adventists Believe,* p. 332.

The Millennium and the End of Sin

Opening Story

"I hate this!" my son cried as he looked up at me with tears streaming down his cheeks. "It's not fair! I hate owies!" The cut on his knee bled enough to scare him, and the pain from the surrounding scratches infuriated my 4-year-old boy so much that in between the crying he erupted into shouts of anger. "I want this to stop! When will it stop hurting, Daddy?"

I could have mentioned to him that the pain-free life he thought he was entitled to did not exist, that his suffering was not an attack on him, but the reality of living in a sin-filled world. In short, I could have said, "Get used to it!"

Before you turn me in to the authorities, know that I would never wish those thoughts on anyone, much less say them to my 4-year-old. Why? Because our Father in heaven has something else in mind for us to "get used to."

As the effects of sin increase around us, the response for believers is not to ignore it, excuse it, evade it, or accept it. God will put an end to the suffering, and He will invite everyone who trusts in His grace to "get used to" a new way—a new way to live, breathe, and grow. The old way will go away. God will make sure of that. But in getting rid of the old way we will need to get used to life the new way.

Jesus describes a time of judgment that will expose sin for what it is and also reveal God's grace in all its fullness as well. He warns people to get serious about sin and about the great plan God has for eliminating it forever.

Life of Christ

Luke 12:1-10

"Meanwhile, when a crowd of many thousands had gathered, so that they were trampling on one another, Jesus began to speak first to his disciples, saying: 'Be on your guard against the yeast of the Pharisees, which is hypocrisy. There is nothing concealed that will not be disclosed, or hidden that will not be made known. What you have said in the dark will be heard in the daylight, and what you have whispered in the ear in the inner rooms will be proclaimed from the roofs. I tell you, my friends, do not be afraid of those who kill the body and after that can do no more. But I will show you whom you should fear: Fear him who, after the killing of the body, has power to throw you into hell. Yes, I tell you, fear him. Are not five sparrows sold for two pennies? Yet not one of them is forgotten by God. Indeed, the very hairs of your head are all numbered. Don't be afraid; you are worth more than many sparrows. I tell you, whoever acknowledges me before men, the Son of Man will also acknowledge him before the angels of God. But he who disowns me before men will be disowned before the angels of God. And everyone who speaks a word against the Son of Man will be forgiven, but anyone who blasphemes against the Holy Spirit will not be forgiven.'"

We Believe

The Millennium and the End of Sin

"The millennium is the thousand-year reign of Christ with His saints in heaven between the first and second resurrections. During this time the wicked dead will be judged; the earth will be utterly desolate, without living human inhabitants, but occupied by Satan and his angels. At its close Christ with His saints and the Holy City will descend from heaven to earth. The unrighteous dead will then be resurrected, and with Satan and his angels will surround the city; but fire from God will consume them and cleanse the earth. The universe will thus be freed of sin and sinners forever."*

    a. Revelation 20

    b. 1 Corinthians 6:2, 3

    c. Jeremiah 4:23-26

    d. Revelation 21:1-5

    e. Malachi 4:1

    f. Ezekiel 28:18, 19

Way to Pray

As you pray, make a list of all the things that you want to talk to God about during the millennium. As God seeks to prepare you for heaven, what sin does He want to put an end to in your life today?

More Than Words

Discuss with someone this week what it might be like when sin will be no more. Try to encourage those who need the hope of a righteous end and then reflect on your experience with that person.

In the Mirror

Reflect on the beauty of the 1,000 years; also spend some time wondering on paper about what it will be like to live without the effects of sin, and write your thoughts on paper.

---

* *Seventh-day Adventists Believe*, p. 362.

The New Earth

Opening Story

"Ahh. This is heaven," my friend said. But it was not heaven to me! We were in a small sailboat out on the ocean, and the only thing that remotely resembled anything lovely was the security of the life vest I clutched. I'm not much of a water person, but my friend could think of no other place on earth he'd rather be than *stranded out on the ocean with no wind, no food, no solid ground!*

Although I have never been to heaven, I was certain that this was not it. But what is heaven, and what will it really be like? The images of harps and clouds, of people with wings floating around like celestial butterflies, are not biblical—nor are they something we all would say "This is heaven" to. What will heaven be like? is a popular question but a dangerous one. The only way to even begin to try to give an answer is to make comparisons—or contradictions. The apostle John tells us what heaven will not be like. Revelation 21:4 describes heaven as having "no more death or mourning or crying or pain."

If you were to describe "heaven," how would you do it?

The new earth is a better way to see God's original hope for humanity. When we think of Paradise we don't imagine cloud-enshrined condos—we conjure up a real place. But how real is Paradise?

Ask the thief on the cross. Jesus gives him a personal invitation to the good life. Watch and see:

Life of Christ

Luke 23:39-43

"One of the criminals who hung there hurled insults at him: 'Aren't you the Christ? Save yourself and us!' But the other criminal rebuked him. 'Don't you fear God,' he said, 'since you are under the same sentence? We are punished justly, for we are getting what our deeds deserve. But this man has done nothing wrong.' Then he said, 'Jesus, remember me when you come into your kingdom.' Jesus answered him, 'I tell you the truth, . . . you will be with me in paradise.'"

We Believe

The New Earth

"On the new earth, in which righteousness dwells, God will provide an eternal home for the redeemed and a perfect environment for everlasting life, love, joy, and learning in His presence. For here God Himself will dwell with His people, and suffering and death will have passed away. The great controversy will be ended, and sin will be no more. All things, animate and inanimate, will declare that God is love, and He shall reign forever. Amen."*

- **a.** 2 Peter 3:13
- **b.** Isaiah 35
- **c.** Isaiah 65:17-25
- **d.** Matthew 5:5
- **e.** Revelation 21:1-7; 22:1-5; 11:15

Way to Pray

Meditate on the creative power of Christ and pray about the parts of your life that you want God to re-create. What do you want to be new in your heart today?

More Than Words

Isaiah tells us that in the new earth we will plant vineyards—that is, do normal, everyday stuff. It seems as though we can have some real, tangible ideas about how we will live in the new earth. Place a seed or put a flower in the yard or in your window as a symbol of your hope for the new earth. Not only does it remind you of the joy to come; it furthers your faith experience and hopefully deepens the reality of the new earth in your mind.

In the Mirror

Reflect on how the new earth relates to the plan of salvation.

* *Seventh-day Adventists Believe*, p. 374.

Stewardship

Open Questions

Rank in order (1—the greatest sacrifice; 5—the least)
In my life the greatest sacrifice for me to give would be:

____ Money

____ Time for church work

____ Talents for service

____ My energy for good causes

____ Opinions and preconceived ideas

Opening Story

"A long time ago a very godly and generous businessman in London was asked for a donation for a charitable project. Very little was expected because the businessman had recently sustained a heavy loss from the shipwreck of some of his ships. To the amazement of the leaders of the charity, he gave about ten times as much as he was expected to give to the project. When asked how he was able to give so much in light of his business difficulties the businessman replied, 'It is quite true, I have sustained a heavy loss by these vessels being wrecked, but that is the very reason why I give you so much; for I must make better use than ever of my stewardship lest it should be entirely taken from me.'"[1]

While I'm not sure whether the man gave from fear of losing everything or from a real conviction that his stewardship could glorify God, the point is well made. Mark it down as a truth for eternity—God is the great giver and selfless sacrificer (if that can be considered a word), and He expects His children to follow suit. There are many ways to give, and Christians are challenged to be selfless in all of them, not just some. Money, time, talents, energy, passion, interests, relationships, possessions, reputation—they are all areas that can speak plainly of Christ's gracious and selfless love. Apparently, the woman at the Temple figured it out.

Life of Christ

Mark 12:41-44

"Jesus sat down opposite the place where the offerings were put and watched the crowd putting their money into the temple treasury. Many rich people threw in large amounts. But a poor widow came and put in two very small copper coins, worth only a fraction of a penny. Calling his disciples to him, Jesus said, 'I tell you the truth, this poor widow has put more into the treasury than all the others. They all gave out of their wealth; but she, out of her poverty, put in everything—all she had to live on.'"

We Believe

Stewardship

"We are God's stewards, entrusted by Him with time and opportunities, abilities and possessions, and the blessings of the earth and its resources. We are responsible to Him for their proper use. We acknowledge God's ownership by faithful service to Him and our fellowmen, and by returning tithes and giving offerings for the proclamation of His gospel and the support and growth of His church.

Stewardship is a privilege given to us by God for nurture in love and the victory over selfishness and covetousness. The steward rejoices in the blessings that come to others as a result of his faithfulness."[2]

- **a.** Genesis 1:26-28; 2:15
- **b.** 1 Chronicles 29:14
- **c.** Haggai 1:3-11
- **d.** Malachi 3:8-12
- **e.** 1 Corinthians 9:9-14
- **f.** Matthew 23:23
- **g.** 2 Corinthians 8:1-15
- **h.** Romans 15:26, 27

Way to Pray

As you pray this week, make a list of all the things that are precious to you and give them to God one by one for His service. Acknowledge the "what's mine is mine" attitudes you may have held and trust God with your whole life.

Consider a prayer that gives God your future: career, spouse, college, etc. . . .

More Than Words

Interview someone who has children in college or older children. Ask the following questions:

When in your life has God come through miraculously for you as a result of your faithful giving?

Why do you think it is hard for us to consider our things or even time as belonging to God and not to ourselves?

What words of wisdom do you have for someone my age about giving and working in the church?

In the Mirror

Reflect on and write about the things you would lay your life down for. What would you surrender the work of the gospel for?

[1] Michael Green, *1500 Illustrations for Biblical Preaching,* pp. 162, 163.
[2] *Seventh-day Adventists Believe,* p. 268.

Christian Behavior

Opening Story

Below New York City live people who have, for one reason or another, chosen to dwell in the sewers. The homeless, the mentally ill, the broken, the outcasts, the has-beens, the addicts, the mindless, the misfits—they huddle beneath the streets of one of the world's most famous cities.

Jennifer Toth, a reporter, studied those who dwelt in the tunnels. In her book *The Mole People* she cites an interchange with a man who let her interview him in exchange for a free lunch:

Flacko, a would-be leader underground, said, "If I was in charge I'd put up a big sign on a platform saying, 'C'mon down! Everyone welcome! Come live free—rent-free, tax-free, independent, free like Mandela!'"

"When he stops smiling, he turns earnest and leans over our table in the Chinese restaurant . . . 'If you write this book,' he says, 'you tell them the tunnels rob you of your life. No one should come down here . . . everyone down here knows it. They won't say it, but they know it.'"[1]

Sounds like the game of the deceiver, doesn't it? Jesus said, "The thief comes only to steal and kill and destroy; I have come that they may have life, and have it to the full" (John 10:10).

God's hope is that others will see His glory in us—the way we live, the way we work, and the way we play. But the question "How do we then live?" has not been a popular one lately, because many think that God's challenge to live holy lives contradicts the message of grace. That if salvation is free, we don't have to do anything in response to God's gift.

Look at the passages of Scripture that describe the kind of life God wants us to live. The underworld and the lies that promote a "better way" are loud and compelling, but Christ won't play that game. He won't seduce us into an addiction. Have you seen the bumper sticker that declares "Addicted to Jesus"? Wrong Jesus. Addictions are a form of slavery. They rob your will of its strength by making it seemingly impossible to choose otherwise. But that's not Jesus. Honesty, purity, faithfulness, wholeness, beauty, and joy are a few of the many life experiences that Christ calls every believer to experience. And another one is obedience. Can you imagine Christ—knowing how much you mean to Him—wanting anything less than the best for you? Not a chance.

Most people know it. Scripture makes the alternatives clear. Look in the Bible and see for yourself.

Life of Christ

Matthew 5:13-15

"'You are the salt of the earth. But if the salt loses its saltiness, how can it be made salty again? It is no longer good for anything, except to be thrown out and trampled by men. You are the light of the world. A city on a hill cannot be hidden. Neither do people light a lamp and put it under a bowl. Instead they put it on its stand, and it gives light to everyone in the house. In the same way, let your light shine before men, that they may see your good deeds and praise your Father in heaven.'"

We Believe

Christian Behavior

"We are called to be a godly people who think, feel, and act in harmony with the principles of heaven. For the Spirit to re-create in us the character of our Lord we involve ourselves only in those things which will produce Christlike purity, health, and joy in our lives. This means that our amusement and entertainment should meet the highest standards of Christian taste and beauty. While recognizing cultural differences, our dress is to be simple, modest, and neat, befitting those whose true beauty does not consist of outward adornment but in the imperishable ornament of a gentle and quiet spirit. It also means that because our bodies are the temple of the Holy Spirit, we are to care for them intelligently. Along with adequate exercise and rest, we are to adopt the most healthful diet possible and abstain from the unclean foods identified in the Scriptures. Since alcoholic beverages, tobacco, and the irresponsible use of drugs and narcotics are harmful to our bodies, we are to abstain from them as well. Instead, we are to engage in whatever brings our thoughts and bodies into the discipline of Christ, who desires our wholesomeness, joy, and goodness."[2]

a. Romans 12:1, 2

b. 1 John 2:6

c. Ephesians 5:16-26

d. Philippians 4:8

e. 1 Peter 3:1-4

f. 1 Corinthians 6:19, 20

g. Leviticus 11

h. 3 John 2

Way to Pray

Be honest with God in prayer about the parts of your life that do not seem to be what God would like for us. Talk openly with Him about the way you feel about the changes that you sense He's asking you to make.

More Than Words

Share the commitments or decisions you have made to live according to God's dreams for you with your partner or with a friend who will help you and remind you of your choice.

In the Mirror

Reflect on what you think this whole topic of living abundantly has to do with God's plan of salvation. How does living lives that are holy relate to what happened at Calvary?

[1] Jennifer Toth, *The Mole People,* p. 233.
[2] *Seventh-day Adventists Believe*, p. 278.

Marriage and Family

Opening Story

The small round breakfast table sat trapped between the angry couple. Although only a few feet separated the two, it seemed as though they were looking at each other from the opposite ends of one of those long royal banquet tables where you can barely see the person at the other end. Gloria and Ron were seemingly at the end of their marriage. It had slowly eroded away for 23 years, and now all they had to talk about was the way each of them felt about their own needs and how they had not been met.

The failure and fall of many relationships have their roots in a preoccupation with self: my needs, my rights, my expectations, my feelings. The opposite is true in growing marriages: my responsibility is to fulfill the needs of my spouse—the needs I promised to meet. Robert Orben alludes to this principle:

"We begin marriage, hoping for fulfillment, but often find frustration. Our own immature neurotic traits are magnified by the fact that the marriage partner has another set of neurotic tendencies. Instead of seeking fulfillment for ourselves, the primary goal should be to fulfill the needs of one's partner. It is thus that our own needs are met."

While a marriage is more than just meeting the other person's needs (remember that Christ alone can satisfy some of them), it seems that the breakdown of marriage begins with "self" becoming the priority. The opposite is also true: when the other person is primary to you, most of your own frustrations fade into the background.

Many have given up on this sacred union that began in Eden. It seems as though they look at marriage only tentatively or with a certain amount of resignation. How do you and I foster a sense of honor for this beautiful relationship? It starts when we are young. But most of all, it begins with the way we love God first. You see, to love another person with your own human, sinful problems makes for an incomplete experience—one that does not always end well. But to love God first and fully—that experience alone makes you a prize for marriage. To know Christ is the best preparation for marriage.

Ask Ron and Gloria. That is where they started after decades of growing apart. They began with Christ. As they looked upon the Savior their hearts turned from their inward focus to each other. They learned to love each other, not with the romantic fury of adolescent lovers, but with a new, real, Godlike love that has made a world of difference in their marriage.

As we consider marriage, notice that even in the day of Christ the struggle to maintain one was real. We find a lot of bickering and arguing over the rules of divorce and remarriage, and most of the arguments missed the mark of what they should have discussed—not how we should divorce, but how we can learn to love the way God intended.

Life of Christ

Matthew 19:1-9

"When Jesus had finished saying these things, he left Galilee and went into the region of Judea to the other side of the Jordan. Large crowds followed him, and he healed them there. Some Pharisees came to him to test him. They asked, 'Is it lawful for a man to divorce his wife for any and every reason?' 'Haven't you read,' he replied, 'that at the beginning the Creator "made them male and female," and said, "For this reason a man will leave his father and mother and be united to his wife, and the two will become one flesh"? So they are no longer two, but one. Therefore what God has joined together, let man not separate.' 'Why then,' they asked, 'did Moses command that a man give his wife a certificate of divorce and send her away?' Jesus replied, 'Moses permitted you to divorce your wives because your hearts were hard. But it was not this way from the beginning. I tell you that anyone who divorces his wife, except for marital unfaithfulness, and marries another woman commits adultery.' "

We Believe

Marriage and Family

"Marriage was divinely established in Eden and affirmed by Jesus to be a lifelong union between a man and a woman in loving companionship. For the Christian, a marriage commitment is to God as well as to the spouse, and should be entered into only between partners who share a common faith. Mutual love, honor, respect, and responsibility are the fabric of this relationship, which is to reflect the love, sanctity, closeness, and permanence of the relationship between Christ and His church. Regarding divorce, Jesus taught that the person who divorces a spouse, except for fornication, and marries another, commits adultery. Although some family relationships may fall short of the ideal, marriage partners who fully commit themselves to each other in Christ may achieve loving unity through the guidance of the Spirit and the nurture of the church. God blesses the family and intends that its members shall assist each other toward complete maturity. Parents are to bring up their children to love and obey the Lord. By their example and their words they are to teach them that Christ is a loving disciplinarian, ever tender and caring, who wants them to become members of His body, the family of God. Increasing family closeness is one of the earmarks of the final gospel message."*

a. Genesis 2:18-25

b. Matthew 19:3-9

c. 2 Corinthians 6:14

d. Ephesians 5:21-33

    e. Matthew 5:31, 32
    f. Exodus 20:12
    g. Ephesians 6:1-4
    h. Proverbs 22:6

Way to Pray

Speak to God openly about your hopes and fears about marriage. Tell Him specifically about how you want Him to be involved in the choosing of a marriage partner. Make some decisions in prayer this week and commit them to God, then share them with your study partner.

More Than Words

Write a letter to your mate (you don't have to have a name yet, or a real person). Describe what you want your marriage to be like and what you are willing to commit yourself to. You might include in your letter your commitment to purity from now until that time. Perhaps you would like to reveal your deepest hopes for your relationship. Such a letter is not a waste of time. Keep the letter—let it remind you of the promises you make to honor God and your future spouse—even though you don't know who he or she is yet.

In the Mirror

Reflect on how the marriage relationship relates to the whole plan of salvation. How does marriage show us God's desire to relate to us?

* _Seventh-day Adventists Believe_, p. 294.

Christ's Ministry in the Heavenly Sanctuary

Opening Story

"I said I was sorry!"

"That's great, Troy. Now all you have to do is find a way to pay for the damage."

"Pay for the damage! I don't have that kind of money. How can I pay for the damage? I said I was sorry—isn't that enough?"

"Actually, no. In this case 'sorry' isn't enough. 'Sorry' and $68 is enough, however, and I'm wondering if you have thought about what you might do to raise the money."

How could they be that heartless? My father and the next-door neighbor were being completely unreasonable—and, I might add, downright unchristian. Where was their compassion? Where was their grace and forgiveness? Whatever happened to "forgive and forget"? Instead, it felt more like "forgiveness when you pay the debt!" Does that sound very biblical?

Think about these scenarios:

A jury finds a man guilty of raping and murdering six teenage girls. In court he announces, "I admit to doing these awful crimes, and I'm very, very sorry. I promise to never do it again."

"The court recognizes your guilt and your admission," the judge declares, "and as long as you promise never to do it again, you may go."

How does that sound? Does it seem like grace to you? No? Why do you so desperately want justice? Isn't forgiveness enough?

If it is, then why did Jesus have to die on the cross? Why couldn't God just pardon us all? Calvary is a very clear example that God does not tolerate sin. He does not simply wave His hand and make the bad stuff go away. The hard truth of it is that in God's world, if you choose to sin, someone has to pay. But it's a good thing that it's God's world, otherwise that someone would have been you and me.

This is not a New Testament concept—it is as old as sin and as real as the skin on your bones. Yet just as old as the problem is the solution. God, in the ministry of the Old Testament sanctuary, taught the children of Israel what grace really is. It was about blood, payment, death, cleansing, judging, forgiving, changing, healing, trusting, and accepting the grim but wonderful reality that someday a Savior would come—no more lambs—and would pay for our sin.

The grand moment arrived at Calvary. Watch—because as Jesus is fully condemned and put to death for our sin, the curtain of the sanctuary is torn. God judges Jesus as though He were you and me, and He judges you and me as though we were Him.

Life of Christ

Matthew 27:45-54

"From the sixth hour until the ninth hour darkness came over all the land. About the ninth hour Jesus cried out in a loud voice, 'Eloi, Eloi, lama sabachthani?'—which means, 'My God, my God, why have you forsaken me?' When some of those standing there heard this, they said, 'He's calling Elijah.' Immediately one of them ran and got a sponge. He filled it with wine vinegar, put it on a stick, and offered it to Jesus to drink. The rest said, 'Now leave him alone. Let's see if Elijah comes to save him.' And when Jesus had cried out again in a loud voice, he gave up his spirit. At that moment the curtain of the temple was torn in two from top to bottom. The earth shook and the rocks split. The tombs broke open and the bodies of many holy people who had died were raised to life. They came out of the tombs, and after Jesus' resurrection they went into the holy city and appeared to many people. When the centurion and those with him who were guarding Jesus saw the earthquake and all that had happened, they were terrified, and exclaimed, 'Surely he was the Son of God!'"

We Believe

Christ's Ministry in the Heavenly Sanctuary

"There is a sanctuary in heaven, the true tabernacle which the Lord set up and not man. In it Christ ministers on our behalf, making available to believers the benefits of His atoning sacrifice offered once for all on the cross. He was inaugurated as our great High Priest and began His intercessory ministry at the time of His ascension. In 1844, at the end of the prophetic period of 2300 days, He entered the second and last phase of His atoning ministry. It is a work of investigative judgment, which is part of the ultimate disposition of all sin, typified by the cleansing of the ancient Hebrew sanctuary on the Day of Atonement. In that typical service the sanctuary was cleansed with the blood of animal sacrifices, but the heavenly things are purified with the perfect sacrifice of the blood of Jesus. The investigative judgment reveals to heavenly intelligences who among the dead are asleep in Christ and therefore, in Him, are deemed worthy to have part in the first resurrection. It also makes manifest who among the living are abiding in Christ, keeping the commandments of God and the faith of Jesus, and in Him, therefore, are ready for translation into His everlasting kingdom. This judgment vindicates the justice of God in saving those who believe in Jesus. It declares that those who have remained loyal to God shall receive the kingdom. The completion of this ministry of Christ will mark the close of human probation before the Second Advent."*

The elements of the sanctuary outline Christ's ministry to us, not only at Calvary, but today in heaven. Ultimately, the sanctuary was then, and still is, about Jesus.

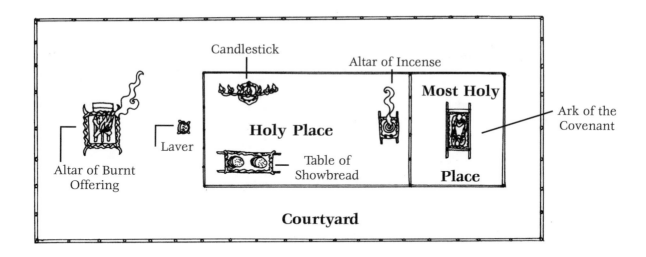

What is the sanctuary?

The courtyard contained the altar of burnt offering and the laver.

The tent of the sanctuary consisted of two parts: the holy place and the Most Holy Place. The holy place housed the seven-branched candlestick (lampstand), the table of showbread, and the altar of incense. The Most Holy Place held the ark of the covenant, which housed the Ten Commandments, which God had written on two tables of stone. Two golden cherubim stood facing each other, and in the middle of the covering was the mercy seat.

What happened?

As a sinner, you would bring a sacrifice (usually a lamb) and place your hands on the innocent animal. The animal was killed as you confessed your sins, in a way taking the sins and placing them on the victim. The priest sprinkled the blood of the animal on the altar of burnt offering or in the holy place. Called the "daily sacrifice," the ritual transferred the sin to the sanctuary. Those who confessed their sins thus walked away forgiven.

Because the sanctuary now contained the sins of the sinner, the high priest would need to cleanse it once a year on the Day of Atonement. On it God judged everyone who had confessed their sins throughout the year. This day was a time of awe and solemn reverence. The high priest chose two goats on the Day of Atonement. One of them he would sacrifice—this was called "the Lord's goat." The other was the scapegoat. The high priest sacrificed the Lord's goat and took its blood into the Most Holy Place. The high priest entered this room only once a year on this special day. He sprinkled the blood on the mercy seat, then returned to the holy place and sprinkled blood on the altar of incense. Finally he moved into the courtyard, where he sprinkled the blood on the altar of burnt offering.

After he finished this, the high priest placed his hands on the head of the other goat (the scapegoat) and confessed the sins of all the people of Israel for the past year and symbolically transferred them to the scapegoat. A Levite took the scapegoat into the wilderness for it to wander around until it died, still bearing the sins of Israel.

What does it mean?

God showed Moses the sanctuary in heaven, and the one Israel's leader then built was a model of the heavenly one. The various parts of the sanctuary have tremendous meaning and purpose. The sanctuary service demonstrates the two parts of Christ's ministry (the work of intercession and the work of judgment).

The First Part (the Courtyard and the Holy Place)

When people confessed their sin over the lamb and it was killed and placed on the altar, it symbolized the sacrifice of Christ as He died on Calvary. (Remember, John the Baptist said, "Behold the Lamb of God who takes away the sins of the world.")

The laver, filled with water, illustrates baptism and the forgiveness of sins as the water washes away the old person of sin.

In the holy place the table of showbread depicts Christ, who is the bread of life (John 6:35). The candlesticks symbolize that Jesus was the light of the world (John 8:12). And the altar of incense stands for the way Christ intercedes for sinners (John 17).

The Second Part (the Most Holy Place)

The ministry of the second compartment involves judgment. The truth about sin is that even though God provides forgiveness for sin, justice demands that someone has to pay. The ark of the covenant is a timeless symbol of God's unchanging law of righteousness. It is important to remember that what makes the sacrifice and the blood and death necessary is God's law. Sin (transgression of the law) brings death. The ark represents God's throne, where His justice calls for an answer to the sin problem.

The scapegoat depicts Satan, whom God banishes from the sanctuary. He bears responsibility for the sins of the people. Justice is served. Sin, death, and shame die with the one who initiated them.

The sanctuary is not a sick ritual of an angry God who wants blood. No, quite the opposite, it lets us witness a loving but just God who deals with the sin problem by becoming the payment for sin. While many stories of God's love are warm and fuzzy, the sanctuary service is not—it is God's love conquering the cold, cruel effects of sin. Although not pretty, it saves.

As you read the passages that describe the heavenly sanctuary and God's plan of salvation, also turn to chapters 23 and 24 in *The Great Controversy* for a more thorough explanation on the work of the sanctuary and Christ's ministry in the sanctuary.

    a. Hebrews 8:1-5; 4:14-16
    b. Daniel 7:9-27; 8:13, 14; 9:24-27
    c. Numbers 14:34
    d. Ezekiel 4:6
    e. Leviticus 16
    f. Revelation 14:6, 7; 20:12; 14:12; 22:12

Way to Pray

In a prayer to God, respond to the truths about your guilt and sin and confidently accept His judgment of you.

More Than Words

This week, not only find a way to forgive someone who has wronged you, but treat them as though they had never wronged you before. It is not forgetting their misdeed, but remembering with mercy.

In the Mirror

Consider how the sanctuary must have helped the children of Israel to understand grace. Also, what are the drawbacks of such a system? Think about how we relate to justice and how and when we demand it. What can you learn from this topic about God's mysterious character?

---

* *Seventh-day Adventists Believe*, p. 312.

The Remnant and the Mission of the Church

"You tell him."

"I don't want to tell him—you tell him."

The argument continued as the two boys tried to decide who would break the news to their father that they had broken the key to the car door in the door lock itself.

I had been sitting in my car waiting for my wife to pick up a few things at the store as I watched the boys race from the front of the store through the parking lot toward the car parked right next to mine.

Although the biggest boy (probably a year or so older) was in the lead, the smaller boy was gaining on him as they made the last few strides to the green station wagon with wood-grained paneled sides. Both obviously trying to get into the front seat, they laughed as they wrestled for position. I couldn't see what happened, but knew the moment that it did. They both stopped and stared at the lock of the driver's side, then glanced at each other. The key had snapped off cleanly in the lock. Now they had to decide who would tell their father about the broken key.

Who will bring the message back to those who need to hear? I have always remembered that experience because of the many times I have had to be the one to bring news. Good news such as "Your mom is out of surgery and is going to be fine," "You passed your class!" or "You have been chosen to be one of our employees!" Then there were times when the news was more than disappointing. "You didn't make the team," or, equally as devastating, "She just wants to be friends." (Who wants to be the bearer of that kind of news?) "I'm sorry, but your brother did not survive the accident."

God's people have never been a majority. Throughout history whole herds of people have rejected God's word, His plan, and His heart's desire. It is often hard to imagine so many people being so utterly oblivious to God's truth. It reminds one of a certain college cross-country race. "At an NCAA cross-country championship held several years ago, the athletes were running along a prescribed route when they stumbled on a perplexing choice. There were apparently two directions that looked reasonable. Unsure of which way to go, the crowded pack began to follow the front runners, who had made their choice. All, that is, except Mike Delcavo. He knew they were going the wrong way, and he tried to convince them of it. As he started running in the opposite direction, and urging the rest to follow him, the majority of the runners ignored him, while others laughed at him. Only four other runners followed Delcavo, while the other 123 runners ran the other way. Out of 128 runners, only Mike and four other runners chose the right direction."[1]

The remnant is a group of people given the responsibility of bringing a message. Its character and content come from God. The chosen people are the instruments by which God delivers that message. The children of Israel had the privilege of declaring the glory and wonder of God to the nations who didn't know of the divine Creator. The role of being a messenger is simple: know what the message is and deliver it.

Jesus stood before His disciples and gave them a similar command. He had a message, and they were to deliver it.

Life of Christ

Matthew 28:19, 20

"Therefore go and make disciples of all nations, baptizing them in the name of the Father and of the Son and of the Holy Spirit, and teaching them to obey everything I have commanded you. And surely I am with you always, to the very end of the age."

How do you think the disciples felt about such a challenge?

With all the trouble the disciples had had before about who was going to be first, with what attitude do you imagine they approached this task? Why?

How would you characterize the special work of the disciples at the end of Jesus' ministry? How would you describe our special task in our world today?

We Believe

The Remnant and the Mission of the Church

"The universal church is composed of all who truly believe in Christ, but in the last days, a time of widespread apostasy, a remnant has been called out to keep the commandments of God and the faith of Jesus. This remnant announces the arrival of the judgment hour, proclaims salvation through Christ, and heralds the approach of His second advent. This proclamation is symbolized by the three angels of Revelation 14; it coincides with the work of judgment in heaven and results in a work of repentance and reform on earth. Every believer is called to have a personal part in this worldwide witness." [2]

    a. Revelation 12:17; 14:6-12; 18:1-4

    b. 2 Corinthians 5:10

    c. Jude 3, 14

    d. 1 Peter 1:16-19

    e. 2 Peter 3:10-14

    f. Revelation 21:1-14

Way to Pray

As you pray, what do you want to invite God to do in your life that will enable you to carry His message? What do you want Him to do *in* you, then *through* you?

More Than Words

Find someone you know or are acquainted with who from your viewpoint loves the Adventist Church's mission. Ask them what it is about the Adventist faith that is most meaningful to them. Why are they a Seventh-day Adventist? What is our role in the last days?

In the Mirror

How do you see your church carrying out its task until Jesus comes? What do you think we need to do more of and what do we need to do less of in order to finish our job?

---

[1] Daniel Schaeffer, *The Bush Won't Burn and I'm All Out of Matches*, p. 67.
[2] *Seventh-day Adventists Believe*, p. 152.

"What's in the Box?"

Spiritual Gifts Survey

Spiritual Gifts Questionnaire for Youth

"What's in the Box?" is a simple approach to finding and practicing our spiritual gifts. The task for the loving and mission-minded church is to ask, "What's in the Box?" In other words, "What is in our kids that can significantly shape and move our church forward—today?"

1. Indicate whether each statement is:

Almost Never	Rarely	Sometimes	Frequently	Almost Always
1	2	3	4	5

For example, a statement might declare "I get really frustrated when I hear people talking about doing something but not doing it."

If you "almost never" feel that way, then you would circle the 1 under "almost never." If you find that you frequently get upset about that, then you would circle number 4.

2. As you answer all the statements, put the number you chose for each question in the light gray area of the column to the right. You should have 10 numbers in each column. Add up the total for each column and write the score in the box at the bottom of the chart.

3. The higher scores are in the areas of the gift you might have. The way to know for sure is to practice using those gifts, and as you have success, you will become more certain about the way God has gifted you.

"We have different gifts, according to the grace given us. If a man's gift is prophesying, let him use it in proportion to his faith. If it is serving, let him serve; if it is teaching, let him teach; if it is encouraging, let him encourage; if it is contributing to the needs of others, let him give generously; if it is leadership, let him govern diligently; if it is showing mercy, let him do it cheerfully" (Romans 12:6-8).

The *ChristWise* approach to spiritual gifts is based on Romans 12:6-8. Some studies on spiritual gifts have up to 24 different spiritual gifts as part of their inventory. For young people, we use the passage in Romans because it simplifies the gifts into seven major categories, which are easier for kids to manage.

The following is a summary of the gifts with a short explanation and an example of what that might look like in a young person.

Prophesy

Speaking the wisdom of God

The term *prophesy* might scare people because it carries all kinds of ideas from calling fire down out of heaven to being able to see into the future. While those experiences may occur, the gift of prophecy has more to do with a person's ability to understand and speak wisely on behalf of God. Individuals who have this gift have the ability to be "in tune" with God in a special way. They tend to be willing to speak up, speak out, and go against the flow of peer pressure. You might see it in the way a young person tries to get people to "do the right thing." We don't want to avoid the possibility that they might see "dreams and visions," but mostly the gift involves courage and character and being really perceptive.

Server

Those who just want to get things done have tremendous value to the church. When God lives in such individuals, great things happen for Him. While some may just want to make plans, helpers make lists of the things to do and get started. They feel best when they are working, and even if the details seem menial, they see how the little parts can fit into the big picture. You can see it in children who always have to be helping, constantly volunteering, and can't sit still for very long.

Teacher/Learner

We combine the gift of teacher/learner because most good teachers love learning. Rarely are teachers effective if they are not teachable themselves. In the church, they like to study and discover truth and also enjoy finding the best ways to communicate it. Such kids not only love it when they understand but they enjoy the way they discovered it and seem to be willing to help others learn.

Builder

Builders have the ability to challenge and strengthen others with their words and deeds. Often called the gift of encouragement, it comes from the idea of building a house. We construct a house step by step, piece by piece. It is obvious as well that while it takes time to build a house, it requires only one stick of dynamite or one earthquake or tornado to utterly destroy it. The same is true with our words and actions. Negative words and actions can destroy quickly, but positive affirmation builds gradually. The builder has a special ability to say the right thing at the right time. Desiring to move people forward with their words and actions, they tend to be positive, proactive people.

Giver

Those who joyfully spend their time, talents, service, and resources for good works we call givers. They don't have to have a lot of money to have this gift—most young people don't. But their sacrificial spirit and generosity tend to stick out. What drives them is not the appearance of being a generous person, but that they just feel so good about helping other people that they are free with their time, their stuff, and their energy.

Leader

People have many different ideas about what really makes someone a leader. The word literally means "to stand before," or "to preside." Some think it is the person who is the loudest. One of the best definitions for leadership is "the ability to influence others." This could go both ways (positive or negative). Have you heard some of the stories great leaders tell about their childhood—all the trouble that they caused? Somehow, though, they were able to influence others. The best leaders are ones who tend to get others involved instead of being the one who does everything themselves. A leader who has to do everything is usually a server in the wrong job.

Compassion

The gift of compassion is the natural inclination to show mercy and to bring help and healing to another person. If someone is lonely, hungry, or hurting, the gift of compassion moves people deep within. Such individuals have to do something about a problem. You can see it in those who react to injustice or unfairness. When there is an opportunity to make a difference, they become a part of the healing. The difference between someone with the gift of compassion and someone who is a server is that compassion sees someone in pain sooner than others.

Questions	Answers					Gifts						
	Almost Never	Rarely	Sometimes	Frequently	Almost Always							
I'm very sensitive to what is good and what is not.	1	2	3	4	5							
I am the first person to jump in and help others.	1	2	3	4	5							
I like to be in charge of people.	1	2	3	4	5							
I can sense when others are hurting, and I reach out to them.	1	2	3	4	5							
I feel that it is my job to provide and continue to give resources to those less fortunate than myself.	1	2	3	4	5							
I want people to work together.	1	2	3	4	5							
I do not like games in which people can lose.	1	2	3	4	5							
I see the Bible as the truth.	1	2	3	4	5							
I want to be appreciated for the tasks I do for others.	1	2	3	4	5							
I have a vision for the future.	1	2	3	4	5							
I don't like to focus on the bad in others.	1	2	3	4	5							
I trust that God will take care of me.	1	2	3	4	5							
I get many tasks done in time.	1	2	3	4	5							
Major decisions are hard for me to make.	1	2	3	4	5							

Questions	Answers					Gifts						
	Almost Never	Rarely	Sometimes	Frequently	Almost Always							
I feel that God directly speaks to me.	1	2	3	4	5	X						
It is easier for me to do things for others than just to listen and talk to them.	1	2	3	4	5		X					
I like new goals and new pursuits.	1	2	3	4	5			X				
I want others to be happy.	1	2	3	4	5				X			
I don't like others to know how much I give of my resources.	1	2	3	4	5					X		
I have a real sense of respect for those older than I.	1	2	3	4	5						X	
I feel best when everyone else is happy.	1	2	3	4	5							X
I want to tell others of what God has said to me.	1	2	3	4	5	X						
I see the needs of others and act on that.	1	2	3	4	5		X					
I respect those who are older than I and those who have more wisdom than I do.	1	2	3	4	5			X				
I don't like to hurt others by my actions or words.	1	2	3	4	5				X			
If I cannot give money or objects, I will give of my time.	1	2	3	4	5					X		
I get along well with people regardless of their age.	1	2	3	4	5						X	

Questions	Answers					Gifts						
	Almost Never	Rarely	Sometimes	Frequently	Almost Always							
When others are hurting I have a hard time thinking about anything else.	1	2	3	4	5							
I can be harsh and blunt when I talk to people.	1	2	3	4	5							
I cannot leave a project until it is completed in the best possible way.	1	2	3	4	5							
I want to work with a good group of people to accomplish a task.	1	2	3	4	5							
I hurt when I see others in pain and sorrow.	1	2	3	4	5							
I love to give of myself and my resources.	1	2	3	4	5							
I feel as if I'm most helpful when I'm in charge.	1	2	3	4	5							
I tend to believe what other people tell me.	1	2	3	4	5							
Sometimes I have a low self-esteem.	1	2	3	4	5							
I prefer to be a follower.	1	2	3	4	5							
I do not let others know when criticism has hurt me.	1	2	3	4	5							
I don't want to be the center of attention.	1	2	3	4	5							
I always give 10 percent of my earnings and then offerings on top of that.	1	2	3	4	5							

Questions	Answers					Gifts
	Almost Never	Rarely	Sometimes	Frequently	Almost Always	
If people don't like me or what I have done, I don't let it upset me.	1	2	3	4	5	
I feel that I can help others by praying.	1	2	3	4	5	
I do not like to be wrong in the opinions I hold.	1	2	3	4	5	
It is easier for me to do a job than find someone to do it.	1	2	3	4	5	
I am good at networking and finding people to help the cause.	1	2	3	4	5	
I enjoy reaching out to those who are sick, or to those who seem upset.	1	2	3	4	5	
I like to cheer people up by what I donate to others.	1	2	3	4	5	
I do not really like to do detailed work.	1	2	3	4	5	
I can't stand it when people fight or are hateful to each other.	1	2	3	4	5	
I want to see others grow deeper in their relationship with Christ.	1	2	3	4	5	
Sometimes I help so much that I don't focus on the spiritual needs of others.	1	2	3	4	5	

Questions	Answers					Gifts
	Almost Never	Rarely	Sometimes	Frequently	Almost Always	
I like my life to be organized.	1	2	3	4	5	
I don't want people to feel left out or alone.	1	2	3	4	5	
My biggest desire is to share with others what Jesus did for them on the cross.	1	2	3	4	5	
Letting others know how I feel comes pretty easy for me.	1	2	3	4	5	
I notice quickly when others feel left out.	1	2	3	4	5	
I know when others speak if their words are from God.	1	2	3	4	5	
I enjoy being hospitable to others.	1	2	3	4	5	
I tend to be a workaholic.	1	2	3	4	5	
I would enjoy going to a poverty-stricken society to reach out to others.	1	2	3	4	5	
I am happy to do without things so that others can live a better life.	1	2	3	4	5	
I like to dream of better ways to get things done.	1	2	3	4	5	
I tend to think of the other person's feelings.	1	2	3	4	5	
I want to be instrumental in sharing the gospel and changing people's lives.	1	2	3	4	5	

Questions	Answers					Gifts						
	Almost Never	Rarely	Sometimes	Frequently	Almost Always							
I am the first to offer my help in a task that needs to be accomplished.	1	2	3	4	5							
I put my heart and soul into the job and organization that I am a part of.	1	2	3	4	5							
I communicate with people on a one-on-one level, not in large groups.	1	2	3	4	5							
I manage money well.	1	2	3	4	5							
I feel as if I have to win when playing a game.	1	2	3	4	5							
I can sense when people are lying to me.	1	2	3	4	5							
TOTALS												
						P	S	T	B	G	L	C

P = Prophesy　　**T = Teacher**　　**G = Giver**　　**C = Compassion**

S = Server　　**B = Builder**　　**L = Leader**

128

Small Group Study Questions for the "Life of Christ" Sections

Lesson 1

John 20:24-31

1. After three years of ministry Christ's message seemingly had not gotten through to people—not just to Thomas, but to many others. While Christ did many wonderful acts of kindness, many of His closest followers still had many questions as to who He was. Why do you suppose that is true?

2. Why do you think Thomas was "not with the disciples" when they first saw Jesus after His resurrection?

3. How long was it before Thomas eventually saw Jesus? Why do you think it took so long for Thomas and Jesus to meet together?

4. What evidence did Thomas and the other disciples have to really know Jesus? Do you think just seeing Christ is enough to know and believe?

5. Do you see yourself as a trusting person or as more skeptical?

6. In John 20:30, 31, what do we have in the way of knowledge about Jesus and what do we not have? According to John, is that enough? Why?

Lesson 2

Matthew 28:18-20

1. What words would you use to describe your human father or mother? Describe one of your parents in 25 words or less.
2. Is this description true? Is it accurate? Is it complete? In what ways is our understanding of God complete/incomplete?
3. How do we live in service to a God we don't know completely?
4. Where do we see evidence of the Trinity throughout the life of Christ? throughout the Bible?
5. How do the "three who are one" relate to Each Other? Are They separate? Do They have different roles and abilities?
6. In your own words, describe what you believe to be true about the Trinity.

Lesson 3

Luke 4:1-13

Mark 8:27-33

Mark 14:32-38

Matthew 27:39-43

1. Why do you think Jesus went into the wilderness? What was His motivation?
2. What is significant about His being there for 40 days?
3. When Satan tempts Jesus, he begins by saying, "If you are the Son of God . . ." Why does he do this, and what is his master plan?

4. What was tempting to Jesus about the three tests? What is the "real" temptation for Jesus? How are these temptations different from what we face? How are they alike?
5. What is significant about the way Jesus responds to the temptations?
6. What other times was Jesus tempted like this?
7. What is the war between good and evil about? What is the temptation Satan constantly throws at Jesus?
8. How would you describe Jesus' response to these dilemmas? With what attitude does He react?
9. In a sentence or two, describe what was God's will as opposed to the will of Jesus in the garden. (When Jesus said, "Not My will, but Yours . . .")
10. What do you think it will take for us (you) to be able to pray that prayer under any circumstance? What circumstance is most difficult for you to surrender your will to God's?

Lesson 4

Mark 1:40-45

1. Whom do you know—or know of—who seems almost unreachable?
2. Who do you think is harder for God to save, those whose sinful lives keep them far away or those who don't think they are that far away from God at all?
3. Describe what you know about lepers in the time of Christ.
4. What is significant about the leper's statement "If you are willing, you can make me clean"? Discuss the leper's attitude about his condition and his confidence in Jesus' abilities.
5. What is the difference between pity, sympathy, and empathy? How does compassion fit into these three words?
6. What do you think is significant about the fact that Jesus "touched" him and said, "I am willing"?
7. Have you considered what that moment of healing must have been like? Share among each other how you envision this miracle occurring?

8. Why do you think Jesus told him to show himself to the priest and go through the ritual of cleansing? Read Leviticus 14:1-9 and see if you can make any connection between this ritual and the meaning of Christ's work on the cross. Is there a connection? Of the two birds, which represents the leper? What does the other bird symbolize?

9. How did the leper's testimony impact the ministry of Christ? Share with your group a time when someone's personal story of conversion had a big effect on your relationship with God.

10. In what ways are we all like the leper, and how does this story reflect Christ's attitudes toward sinners?

11. How is the leper's experience with leprosy and healing like our experience with sin and salvation?

Lesson 5

John 1:10-13

1. Read John 3:1-12. "You are a great teacher from God, and God is with you." How does Nicodemus's understanding of who Jesus is affect the way he talks to Jesus? What if that is all Jesus is: "a teacher sent from God"? Does that change the way he relates to Christ? In what way?

2. Discuss what you think is going on in Nicodemus's heart as he waits until night before visiting Jesus. What kind of person do you think he might be?

3. What role do miraculous signs play in authenticating Jesus' ministry? Do His miracles dispel any doubts about His being Messiah?

4. How would you define the kingdom of God? What is a kingdom?

5. What do you think it means to be born again? As you look at Nicodemus's response, why do you think he is having such trouble understanding what Jesus is talking about?

6. Consider the statement "Spiritual things are spiritually discerned" (see 1 Corinthians 2:14).

7. What do you think Jesus is referring to when He says, "Born of water and the Spirit" (John 3:5)?

8. Why is the "wind blowing" a good metaphor for the work of the Holy Spirit in a person's life? Share a moment from your own experience when the Spirit quietly spoke to you and worked with you in a private, personal way.

9. After reading John 1:10-13, discuss the basic steps to becoming born of God, or born again.

10. Think of a time in your relationship with God that you became new. What prompted your surrender? How did you respond?

11. "Born, not of human will or human decision, but born of God." When you think of the word "adoption," how does this concept fit in with the new-birth experience? In what way is baptism a rebirth experience that is different from normal birth?

Lesson 6

John 1:1-14

1. When have you called out to someone in public, only to find out the individual was not who you thought he or she was? What happened?

2. What is significant about the fact that Jesus was the active agent at Creation (Colossians 1:13-16; Hebrews 1:1, 2)?

3. Why do you think John starts his Gospel the way he does? Compare his opening statement with the opening statements of the other Gospels. Next, look at the beginnings of 1 John and the book of Revelation and see what you discover.

4. The phrase "In him was life" (John 1:4) is powerful. How do we see this idea played out in the life of Jesus? Give a few examples of how you believe Jesus demonstrated this phrase.

5. The phrase "that life was the light of men" (verse 4) is also powerful. How was Christ's life a light for people in those days? How is their darkness like ours today?

6. Explain the meaning of the statement "The Word became flesh and made his dwelling among us. We have seen his glory" (verse 14). How does it relate to the creation of the world? Also explain this statement in light of the sanctuary of the Old Testament (Exodus 29:45, 46; 24:16; 40:34).

7. How do you see the two attributes "grace and truth" demonstrated in Jesus' life?

Lesson 7

Matthew 22:34-40

1. Share a time in your life when someone asked you a "loaded question." How did you respond?
2. How would you have answered the question that the expert in law posed to Jesus? Which commandment would you have chosen? Why?
3. Whom do you know who seems to love God "with all their heart, all their soul, and all their mind"? How has their life influenced yours?
4. Why do you think Jesus quoted Deuteronomy 6:4-6 instead of one of the Ten Commandments? What does His response tell us about how to relate to God's law?
5. When have you had a moment in which you felt as if you "loved God with all your heart, soul, and strength"? Describe what was happening in your life at that time.
6. How does Jesus completely avoid the meaningless question and answer the meaningful one?
7. "All the Law and the Prophets hang on these two commandments" basically says that the entire Old Testament is God's law. Brainstorm about some of the famous stories and passages of the Old Testament and put them under the category of one of the two commandments.

Lesson 8

Luke 13:10-16

1. Can you think of a time in your life when another's hypocrisy infuriated you?
2. When have you ever "majored in minors" or focused on the unimportant rather than the most important?

3. Discuss what this woman's condition might look like today?

4. What do you think people thought would be the source of her illness?

5. When Jesus saw her, He set her free. For 18 years she was in misery. What is significant about the way Jesus "sees" people and "frees" them? How does the Sabbath fit with this idea?

6. When the leaders were "indignant" because Jesus healed on the Sabbath, what thoughts went through your head as you read their words? How did you feel?

7. Do you think Jesus considered healing "work"? Even if He did, do you think it would have changed His response? Why/Why not?

8. How does the analogy of the ox/donkey and the "daughter of Abraham" explore the motives of the religious leaders?

9. If, for Jesus, Sabbath is about seeing and freeing people, how would your Sabbaths change if you were to follow that example?

Lesson 9

Read the passage or passages (as a group or in pairs, each pair having one passage).

Matthew 9:11-13

Matthew 20:20-28

Luke 19:5-10

Matthew 5:17, 18

Reflect on the following questions:

1. What is happening in each passage that prompts Jesus to make a statement?

2. What does Jesus say He came to do/be?

3. How do you see this fulfilled in specific moments of His life and ministry?

4. Read John 20:30, 31 and 21:24, 25. What does this say about the stories from the life of Christ we have? And what does it say about the many stories we don't have? What is the purpose of the stories about His life?

5. C. S. Lewis said, "A man who was merely a man and said the sort of things Jesus said wouldn't be a great moral teacher. He'd either be a lunatic—on the level with a man who says he's a poached egg—or else he'd be the devil of hell. You must make your choice. Either this man was, and is, the Son of God, or else a madman or something worse." How do you respond to this statement? On what basis is this statement true?

Lesson 10

Mark 14:17-26

1. What holiday most reminds you of what God intended the day to celebrate? What aspect seems to have become obscured the most?

2. Describe the most memorable Communion service you have ever attended and participated in.

3. When Jesus announced the betrayal of one of the disciples, how do you think it changed the mood of everyone present? Why do you think betrayal receives such a stern rebuke: "It would be better if they were never born"?

4. What is the meaning given to the emblems (bread and the wine) in the Last Supper?

5. When Jesus promises that He will wait until He comes again to eat and drink this meal with us, how does this statement make the Communion service more sacred?

6. How can you experience the blessings of God's grace at Communion both personally and as a church? What are some ways you can deepen the importance and meaning of this experience in your church?

Lesson 11

Luke 10:1-20

1. When have others asked you to do something you thought you were unqualified or untrained to do? Share your experience.
2. How would you characterize the type of work Christ calls His followers to do? Describe the degree or level of difficulty of the tasks that Jesus challenged the disciples with.
3. What preparation did they have? What skills did they need the most for this task?
4. Why do you think Jesus sent them out two by two?
5. When Jesus says, "He who rejects you rejects me," what does this say about the nature of the ministry He calls disciples to? How do you relate to rejection?
6. When the disciples returned from their work they shared all their experiences with joy. Did you think they all succeeded? What stories did they tell?
7. "Christ calls us to be faithful, not successful." How does this phrase relate to the above story? How much of our behavior as Christians depends on the reactions of others?

Lesson 12

Matthew 16:13-18

1. Who is a person in your church who would be sorely missed if they should leave? Why? (Don't use pastors as an example.)
2. What metaphor or symbol would you use to describe your church? Why did you choose the symbol you selected?
3. What do you think Jesus was trying to teach with such questions about His identity?
4. "Who do you say I am?" Is this a question for the disciples or just Peter? Why?

5. How much do you think the disciples really knew about who Jesus was?

6. How do you think God revealed this knowledge to Peter?

7. "You are Peter, and on this rock I will build my church." The statement has started a lot of arguments in the past. We can interpret it in several ways. Think about which one makes the most sense to you: (1) The rock Jesus refers to is Himself—not Peter. Jesus is simply saying, "You are Peter [a little stone]" but on "this rock," pointing to Himself, "I will build my church." (2) The rock is Peter's confession of Jesus as Lord, signifying that on the testimonies of believers the foundation is built. (3) The rock is Peter, and here begins the reign of papal supremacy. (4) The rock is Peter, and Jesus is simply saying that the church is going to be built on people, people who testify to "who I am."

8. Look at Acts 2:44-47 and imagine your church living like this. What would happen to your community if your church began to do such things? What would it take to cause this kind of revolution? Is that something you are interested in?

Lesson 13

Read the passage or passages (as a group or in pairs, each pair having one passage).

John 11:1-44

Mark 5:35-43

Luke 7:11-17

1. When in your life has the fear of death been very real to you? How did you resolve your fear?

2. With what attitude does Jesus approach the scene of death? How does He behave toward the loved ones and the deceased?

3. What does it mean that with one word, one breath, one touch Jesus overcomes death? How does this kind of Savior draw people?

4. Why do you think the Gospels include these three stories? What do they say about God, death, resurrection, and hope that is not mentioned in the other stories?
5. How does the one who trusts in Christ respond to death? Even though we believe, do we not still have fears? How do we then live?

Lesson 14

John 14:1-20

1. When in your life has someone promised you something you thought was impossible to deliver?
2. How well do you think the disciples understood the mission of Jesus? What are some of the parts of His life and ministry that they might have found hard to believe?
3. The disciples are obviously anxious and troubled about the way Jesus is talking. Why do you think they became uncomfortable when He mentioned leaving?
4. "I will come again and receive you to Myself." Even in light of passages that speak of a deep abiding relationship, why does the second coming of Jesus strike a certain amount of fear even in the minds of believers?
5. Note the verses that describe the role of the Holy Spirit in our lives while we work and wait for His return. What does the work of the Holy Spirit have to do with the second coming of Christ?
6. How does our attitude about the Second Coming differ from that of the disciples who heard these words straight from the lips of Jesus?
7. Consider the message of the second coming of Christ. How foreign is it to the world we live in? Do you think people today are interested or willing to hear about such things? Why or why not?
8. Practice the presence of the Holy Spirit this week. What are some practical ways to be mindful of God's Spirit in your life?

Lesson 15

Luke 12:1-10

1. When have you thought that someone's motives were pure, only to find out that they had deceived you? How did you feel? Do such experiences make us skeptical or suspicious?
2. Why do you think it is so difficult to discern another person's motivation?
3. Spend a few minutes talking about what is happening around this passage, as well as the circumstances of Jesus' words to His disciples. How does the frantic scene add to the hard things Jesus says in this story?
4. What verses or phrases seem to speak to you about the authenticity and the sincerity of people's hearts?
5. Discuss the serious way in which Jesus warns the disciples of the issues of deception, judgment, and loyalty. Where do you see these themes discussed in this passage (deception, judgment, loyalty), and what does Jesus say about them?
6. How do you explain the harsh nature of Christ (verses 4 and 5) and in the same breath words of comfort, hope, and affirmation (verses 6 and 7)?
7. To Christ, how important is our public confession of Him? How does our confession of Christ now affect His relationship to us?
8. People are complex beings. When Christ finally ends sin, sinners, and Satan by fire, how will we know God was true, just, and right in His punishment?

Lesson 16

Luke 23:39-43

1. "First impressions aren't always correct." How has this been true for you? When have you had

to change your mind about someone after learning more about them?

2. As the two thieves are crucified with Jesus, is their initial hostility toward Christ something you might expect? How does the statement "Aren't you the Christ? Save yourself and us!" contradict the very purpose of Christ dying on Calvary?

3. How would you characterize the request of the converted thief? Bold? Presumptuous? A shot in the dark? Explain.

4. In what ways is our experience similar to that of the thief on the cross? How is it different?

5. Paradise—do you think that when the thief hears these words he is thinking about trees and waterfalls, with bunnies hopping freely around in a cool green meadow? What do you think "Paradise" means to this man who has just been handed this gift?

6. What does Paradise mean for us?

Lesson 17

Mark 12:41-44

1. What is your favorite place to go just to watch people? Why?

2. Have you ever caught someone doing an act of kindness who thought they were not being watched? What happened?

3. Think about your state of mind when you give at church. How would you describe your attitude?

4. Compare the givers in this story. In Christ's mind, what would it take for the rich to give as much as the widow?

5. Think about the different ways people can be tremendously wealthy as well as poverty-stricken. In what ways are you wealthy, and in what ways are you poor? How is an awareness of the two helpful in your walk with God?

6. Whom do you know who is a "giver" like this widow (not necessarily in money, but in time, talents, energy, love)?

7. Why do you think the Gospels include this story? What truths do you think it teaches?

8. How do you think you will be different because of your study of this passage?

Lesson 18

Matthew 5:13-15

1. Who would you say has had the most influence on you as a Christian? Why?

2. Why are lifestyle and personal choices such a hot debate in Christian churches?

3. Why is salt a powerful metaphor for Christian living? What attributes of salt make it useful for others?

4. Why is light a powerful metaphor for Christian living? What attributes of light make it useful for others?

5. What would change in your lifestyle if you used the ideas "salt" and "light" to gauge every decision you made? "Am I a light to this world when I . . . ?"

6. Get specific with your partner or group about how you can apply the concepts of salt and light to your lifestyle. Set some goals for this week to be "salt" and "light" in specific scenarios.

Lesson 19

Matthew 19:1-9

1. Think of three married couples you admire (at least one with children). Why did you choose those three? In one word, describe each marriage.

2. Here again, the Pharisees ask an insincere question. How does Jesus turn their trick question into a teachable moment?

3. Jesus clearly states that marriage is about two people becoming one. Talk about the different ways this applies to the marriage relationship (two becoming one).

4. What is significant about the statement "What God has joined together . . ."?

5. How is the reason that God permitted divorce in the Old Testament because of "the hardness of their hearts" the same today? In what way is it different?

6. What should be the Christian response to marriages that fall apart? How should people be a source of help? What should the church do?

7. What are some personal goals you have as you prepare yourself to be a godly partner for marriage?

Lesson 20

Matthew 27:45-54

1. When in your life have you felt that God was far away?

2. When in your life have you sensed His closeness the most?

3. When Jesus cried out, "Why have you forsaken me?" was it true that God had left Him? If so, why? Or did Jesus just feel abandoned even though God still remained close by? What does this heart-wrenching plea signify for Jesus as well as for us?

4. What do you think the Temple curtain being torn in two really means?

5. What do you think made the difference for the centurion in his attitude toward Christ? What caused him to change his mind about who Jesus was?

6. Read Matthew 1:23; 18:20; and 28:20. What phrase or idea seems to repeat itself throughout the book of Matthew? How does the life of Christ demonstrate the purpose of God's plan to build a sanctuary (Exodus 29:45, 46)?

Lesson 21

Matthew 28:19, 20

1. How do you think the disciples felt about such a challenge?
2. With all the trouble the disciples had had before about who was going to be first, with what attitude do you imagine they approached this task? Why?
3. How would you characterize the special work of the disciples at the end of Jesus' ministry?
4. How would we describe our special work in our world today?
5. What specific ministries and projects do you think you can do that will contribute to finishing God's mission on earth?